RE-PRIVAT
AFTER THE

RE-PRIVATISING WELFARE: AFTER THE LOST CENTURY

Arthur Seldon • Professor P.M. Jackson
Professor E.G. West • Dr David G. Green
Professor Martin Ricketts • Professor Michael Beenstock
Dr Charles Hanson • George Yarrow
Dr Dennis O'Keeffe • Dr Nigel Ashford

Edited by
Arthur Seldon

Institute of Economic Affairs
1996

First published in October 1996

by

THE INSTITUTE OF ECONOMIC AFFAIRS
2 Lord North Street, Westminster, London SW1P 3LB

IEA Readings 45
All rights reserved

ISSN 0305-814X
ISBN 0-255 36384-2

Printed in Great Britain by
Redwood Books, Trowbridge, Wiltshire

Text set in Times Roman 11 on 12 point

CONTENTS

PREFACE

'History is not merely what happened; it is what happened in the context of what might have happened.'

Hugh Trevor-Roper, Regius Professor of History
(Valedictory Address, University of Oxford)

The Original Hopes

The welfare state has been the subject of increasingly exhaustive discussion and closely contested debate between economists, sociologists and political scientists. In recent years doubts have emerged on whether the original egalitarian purposes of its founders can be sustained when there is growing rejection of the high taxes required to pay for them and rising incomes enable more people to buy better services in the market. The original hopes were broadly, in the four main services, high and rising standards in education, the best medical care for all (a utopian but politically tempting vision), housing at low rents for people with low incomes, pensions to maintain the standards of living in retirement for all.

A Defective Outcome

Such hopes have been disappointed and the defects are becoming increasingly apparent. The political process has a short electoral time-scale: government responds to current dissatisfactions, well-founded or not. It is resigned to placate the organised interests of regional or local managements and national trade unions of employees. And the contest between the political parties preserves and inflates the system: the anxiety of the party in power to display its compassion for the 'deprived' prompts its claims to spend more on the welfare state than the party in Opposition. Expenditure is expected to be taken as a measure of effectiveness.

The parties may differ at House of Commons question-time or in the more gentle debates between former Ministers in the House of Lords, but there is a tacit conspiracy to maintain the welfare state, where possible, for its party-political advantages. It is still a powerful way to win votes, especially for its producers if no longer for its consumers.

There are no confessions from Prime Ministers at the top or local government councillors at the periphery, or from academic supporters of the welfare state, no expressions of remorse, no apologies for continuing the long procession of flawed state institutions. Yet they continue to deny the people – especially the low-income poor and 'deprived' – the direct control and influence that parents, prospective patients, tenants, and prospective pensioners could be exerting over the schools, the hospitals, the homes, the provisions for income after a life of work.

The Institute's Work on the Welfare State

When, in 1963, the Institute began its revolutionary inquiries into the economics of the welfare state by introducing the central instrument of economic analysis, the pricing mechanism created by the device of a voucher to cover school fees and health insurance, its authors questioned opinion polling that had shown massive – usually around 80 per cent – public support for 'free' welfare since the last war. The pioneering introduction of pricing was recognised by Professor Mark Blaug, the historian of economic thought, who emphasised its importance for social scientists. His verdict should have warned the academics and the scholars:

> 'Economists will recognise immediately that the [IEA] enquiry in effect elicited information about the slope of the demand schedule.'[1]

The findings were a fundamental corrective to the misleading opinion polling since the 1950s. The introduction of pricing showed that people were just as rational about paying for education and medical care as they were about other goods and services. To adapt Milton Friedman's dictum, 'There's no such thing as a free lunch', research published by the Institute demonstrated that 'There's no such thing as demand without a price'. The priced surveys[2] revealed that preferences between state and private education and medical care varied with their prices. But sociologists, opinion pollsters, and politicians went on ignoring the price factor in public preferences.

The Institute persisted in inquiries into the flawed *rationale* of 'free' state welfare services. In 1964 *Education for Democrats*, written by

---

[1] *Education: A Framework for Choice*, IEA Readings No. 1, London: Institute of Economic Affairs, 1967.

[2] Ralph Harris, Arthur Seldon, *Choice in Welfare*, IEA, 1963, 1965, 1970, 1978, 1987.

Professors Alan Peacock and Jack Wiseman, analysed the economics of a free market in schooling paid for by parents armed with vouchers to create the choices excluded by state education. It then persuaded a young economist, who later blossomed into Professor E.G. West, the leading authority on the genesis of British education, to examine its origins. His *Education and the State* in 1965, with its neglected evidence of considerable self-help by the common people by the 1860s and earlier, provoked disbelief and even condemnation by some historians.

The *Choice in Welfare* surveys in 1965 and 1970[3] had confirmed the 1963 findings. They were followed in 1972 by an examination of the extent and causes of 19th-century 'social deprivation', as the background to the ability of parents to educate or care for their families. *The Long Debate on Poverty*,[4] written by nine historians, similarly caused shock-waves among academics and the *literati* who had long portrayed the welfare state as the indispensable saviour of the working classes. The historians revealed a very different interpretation of the 19th century from the conventional historians and the fiction of Dickens, the Brontes, and other 19th-century novelists.

The defects of the welfare state were creating increasing anxiety in the 1970s. Not least was the false claim of its supporters that it was redistributing income from the rich to the poor. An academic sociologist and political scientist with personal experience of the administration of the welfare services in local government in the North of England, who had become disillusioned and dismayed by its abuses and excesses, had offered the Institute a scholarly account that revealed then little-known defects. It appeared in 1982 as Dr David Green's *The Welfare State: For Rich or for Poor?*, which argued that it redistributed income to the rich from the poor.

Five years later a study by Professor Julian Le Grand and Dr B. Goodin revealed that much the same defect was apparent in the USA and Australia as well as in Great Britain. This is a reversal of the claims for the welfare state that is still not widely understood or accepted by sociologists or politicians.

---

[3] *Choice in Welfare, 1965,* .... *Choice in Welfare, 1970,* Third Report into Knowledge and Preferences in Education, Health Services and Pensions, IEA, 1971.

[4] A. Seldon (ed.), *The Long Debate on Poverty: Essays on Industrialisation and the 'Condition of England'*, IEA Readings No. 9, IEA, 1972, Second Edition, 1974.

The Myth of the Welfare State

The myth continues that, despite its weaknesses and failures, the welfare state is the only way to rescue the poor from the consequences of their poverty. A main reason for this misapprehension is that historians continue to ignore the evidence that the working classes were building their own welfare 'states' long before the Fabians began their outdated teaching in 1884 and the Webbs continued it with Beveridge and Titmuss at the London School of Economics they founded in 1895.

The persistent failure of conventional historians to examine the relevant issues prompted the Institute to publish a Symposium on 'Welfare: The Lost Century' in the October 1994 issue of its journal, *Economic Affairs*, and then to produce this set of *Readings* as a much expanded version of that Symposium. It is timely to supplement the meandering debate on the welfare state as it has developed in academia and politics by a judgement in the light of private provisions in the market – for education, medical care, housing, pensions, and insurance against unemployment – as they were developing before the state replaced them.

The Case for the 'Counter-Factual'

This is the historical method of the 'counter-factual', the study of the history not only of the events that occurred, the institutions that were built, and their disputed results (which academic debate has examined so far) but the potentially more revealing study of the circumstances that explain why they displaced others that were developing with distinct advantages. The richer history of the 'counter-factual' is put simply in the quotation from Professor Lord Dacre (Hugh Trevor-Roper) at the head of this Preface.

The parallel in economic theory is Wieser's 'law of cost' formulated by a founder of the Austrian school of economics, Friedrich von Wieser (1851-1926), that the value of anything is not, as Karl Marx had taught, measured by the value of the labour used in its production, but by the alternatives foregone, the values of the goods and services sacrificed in order to produce it. In this approach, the cost of the welfare state is judged by the value of the welfare services that had been emerging in the market but were repressed or suppressed by the state. The fundamental 'cost' of the welfare state is the schools, the hospitals, the homes, the pensions, the insurance against unemployment and the other welfare services that were developing spontaneously in the mid-to-late-19th century but were gradually almost displaced by the state.

Results of Counter-Factual Analysis

To pursue the counter-factual approach nine economists, political scientists, sociologists, philosophers and historians were invited 'to participate in an effort to stimulate a new way of thinking about the theory and practice of welfare policies'. Their responses constitute the 11 chapters in this volume.

In Chapter 1 Professor Peter Jackson of the University of Leicester opens with a reasoned statement of the case for the welfare state. He sees its limitations, and argues for reforms, but re-asserts in scholarly style the broad general argument that the condition of the people would be 'unthinkable' if it had not been created.

Five essays then cover the main services. Professor E.G. West, formerly of the University of Kent, later of Carleton University in Ottawa, Canada, confirms from further evidence the findings of his original 1965 historical study, *Education and the State*, then dismissed by conventional historians, that there had been substantial development of schooling in Britain long before the state first provided schools in 1870. The evidence had been largely neglected or minimised by historians who had not adequately studied the antecedents of state-provided education. The question for future policy is how they would have developed if they had not been gradually replaced by the 'free' (tax-financed) state schools.

Dr David Green presents parallel evidence for medical care and insurance against ill-health. His researches performed for medical care what Professor West had revealed for education. In both, the state had jumped on 'galloping horses' that would have raced ahead if they had not been hobbled or put out to grass.

Professor Martin Ricketts of Buckingham University describes the market for housing as it has been distorted by government policies on town planning, rent restrictions and other regulations, and how it could be expected to emerge if the distortions were relaxed or removed. He concludes that well-intentioned but not well-considered legislation on housing has on balance harmed the lower-income people they were designed to help. A further aspect of the market for housing, again little discussed in the text-books and popular works by advocates of state subsidies, is that home ownership among the so-called 'artisan classes' was emerging as early as the 1880s in the industrial towns of England.[5]

---

[5] A. Seldon, *Wither the Welfare State*, Occasional Paper 60, London: Institute of Economic Affairs, 1981.

The early forms of unemployment insurance and the scope for their future expansion in the light of his original researches[6] into insurance costs for varying kinds of unemployment are analysed by Professor Michael Beenstock, formerly of the City University Business School, now at the University of Jerusalem. In his view, insurance for unemployment need no longer be controlled by government.

The sixth essay reviews the extent and variety of saving for retirement and other purposes that were expanding from the late-19th century and have lately been urged by government because it will be unable to provide the state pensions it has long promised by 'national insurance'.

In Chapter 7 Dr Charles Hanson of Newcastle University examines the institutions established mostly by working-class people in the spirit of self-help to provide income in sickness and old age. And George Yarrow of the University of Oxford (Chapter 8) analyses the achievements of a main device, the Friendly Societies, and their potential if government now replaced its discrimination against them by opportunities to resume and expand the services they originally developed.

In Chapters 9 and 10 the principles underlying the contrasting supply of welfare by the single mechanisms of the state and in the diverse mechanisms of the market are discussed in two essays. Dr Dennis O'Keeffe argues the economic/sociological merits of 'giving' in its broadest sense in the two systems. Dr Nigel Ashford indicates the political steps required to pass from one system to the other.

Readers are left to draw possibly divergent conclusions from this journey of scholarly imagination by the 10 authors into the services that might now be educating the young, nursing the sick, housing families, and maintaining the retired in their years after a life of earning.

Liberating People from the Welfare State

In our day, there are tentative attempts to liberate the people from the political state, and to return to them the choices and freedoms, the sense of family responsibility and cohesion, and the resulting direct influence their forebears were learning to exert on welfare services. They are fundamentally prompted not so much by political contrition as by the market forces of supply and demand.

---

[6] Michael Beenstock and Valerie Brasse, *Insurance for Unemployment*, London: Allen & Unwin for IEA, 1986; Michael Beenstock and Associates, *Work, Welfare and Taxation*, London: Allen & Unwin, 1987.

Politicians in all parties are recognising for the first time as a profession that their power to continue welfare services as a virtual state monopoly for most people is waning. It is seen most clearly in the growing acceptance by the Opposition of the modest hesitant moves by the Government to create choices in all four main welfare services: the voucher system for nursery schools, not yet to replace 'free' school places but the introduction of the notion of a choice between state and private schools; the 'internal market' in the National Health Service; the sale of local authority housing to its tenants; and, most markedly so far, the encouragement of private saving for retirement.

The Austrian school of economists – notably from Eugen von Bohm-Bawerk in 1914 to the naturalised British Friedrich Hayek in our day – has long taught that the political power of government operates within the ultimately stronger powers of the market that it cannot suppress. Four tendencies will irresistibly undermine the state: rising incomes, advancing technology, resort to some welfare services in Europe, and the mounting rejection of taxes (much larger than is commonly supposed or revealed by official statistics) to finance services increasingly seen as inadequate.

Rising incomes will enable more people down the income scale to escape from inadequate state schools and find ways, by insurance or extended fees, to pay for private schooling. They will insure with competing suppliers to pay for private medicine, not least to avoid the time-wasting queuing and the anxiety-creating long waiting for hospital treatment. Few of the children accustomed to the comforts of air travel to holidays in Spain and beyond will return to live with the petty restrictions imposed on their parents' Council homes. And few will be content to retire on the increasingly precarious state pension.

*   *   *

This book is entitled *Re-Privatising Welfare: After the Lost Century* because, after 100 years, government is being forced to yield its control over welfare to the market. Welfare, in early forms, was being provided by the market from the late 19th century (and earlier), long before it was repressed and almost suppressed by government in 'the welfare state'. Welfare is being '*re*privatised'.

In the late 20th century the market forces of supply (mainly advancing technology) and demand (especially rising incomes) are now at last replacing government. The early private services are returning after 'the Lost Century' – in much advanced form but with the essential same advantages of the market in restoring the power of the consumer in place of the politician.

The book uses the history of 'the Lost Century' to contrast the disadvantages of state welfare of the past against the advantages of the market welfare of the future.

We have to thank Professor Michael Beenstock for his analysis of the 'Lost Century' used in the title.

Arthur Seldon

THE AUTHORS

Arthur Seldon is a Founder President of the IEA and Founder Editor of *Economic Affairs*. His academic interests are the economics of democracy, government, politics, bureaucracy and the increasing tension between government and the market. His main publications are *Pensions in a Free Society*, IEA, 1957; *After the NHS*, IEA, 1968; *The Great Pensions Swindle*, Tom Stacey, 1970; *Capitalism*, Blackwell, 1990; *The State Is Rolling Back*, E. & L. Books and IEA, 1994. He was appointed CBE in 1983. Nominated the first Honorary Fellow, The Mont Pélèrin Society, Vienna, September 1996.

Peter M. Jackson is Professor of Economics and Director of Public Sector Economics Research, University of Leicester, and a member of the IEA's Academic Advisory Council. His main interests are public sector economics and public expenditure analysis. Recent publications are (with C.M. Price) *Privatisation and Regulation* (Longmans, 1994); *Current Issues in Public Finance* (Macmillan, 1993); (with C.V. Brown) *Public Sector Economics* (Blackwell, 1990).

Edwin G. West, who is a member of the IEA's Academic Advisory Council, is Professor Emeritus in the Economics Department at Carleton University, Ottawa. His main areas of interest include public finance, public choice, and the history of economic thought, particularly with respect to the work of Adam Smith. He has written many journal articles in all these areas. His book, *Adam Smith and Modern Economics: From Market Behaviour to Public Choice* (1990), was published by Edward Elgar.

In education, a special American edition of Professor West's pioneering book, *Education and the State* (IEA, London, 1965, Second Edition 1971) was published by the Liberty Fund in 1994. Professor West has also written for the IEA *Economics, Education and the Politician* (Hobart Paper No.42, 1968), and other contributions. His more recent writings include 'The Benthamites as Educational Engineers: The Reputation and the Record' (*History of Political Economy*, Vol.24, No.3, Fall 1992), and 'Education Vouchers in Practice and Principle: A World Survey' (World Bank, HCO working paper 64, February 1996). His most recent paper for the IEA is

Britain's Student Loan System in World Perspective: A Critique (Current Controversies No.9, 1994).

David G. Green is Director of the Health and Welfare Unit, IEA. His main academic interest is the comparative sociology and political science of state and market medical care and welfare. His main publications are *Mutual Aid or Welfare State* (with L. Cromwell), Allen & Unwin, 1984; *Working Class Patients and the Medical Establishment*, Gower-Temple Smith, 1985; *Reinventing Civil Society: The Rediscovery of Welfare without Politics*, IEA Health and Welfare Unit, 1993; *Community Without Politics*, IEA, 1996.

Martin Ricketts is Bernard Sunley Professor of Economic Organisation and Dean of the School of Business at the University of Buckingham. He studied economics at the Universities of Newcastle upon Tyne and York, and was a research economist at the Industrial Policy Group (1970-72) and the Institute of Social and Economic Research at York (1974-77).

Since joining the staff of the University of Buckingham in 1977 he has pursued his interests in public choice, public policy, and the new institutional economics. He was Economic Director of the National Economic Development Office (1991-92). His publications include (with Michael Webb) *The Economics of Energy* (1980), and *The Economics of Business Enterprise* (2nd edn. 1994). He has also published in scholarly journals on government regulation, housing, and other aspects of public policy. Professor Ricketts is the Chairman of the IEA's Academic Advisory Council.

Michael Beenstock is Pinhas Sapir Professor of Economics at the Hebrew University of Jerusalem, Israel, and a member of the IEA's Academic Advisory Council. He was formerly Esmée Fairbairn Professor of Finance and Investment, City University Business School, 1981-87. His principal academic interest is the applied econometric analysis of labour markets, energy, and macro-economic activity. He has published several books including *Insurance for Unemployment* (with Valerie Brasse), Allen & Unwin for the Institute of Economic Affairs, 1986.

Charles G. Hanson retired in 1995 from his post as Senior Lecturer in Economics at the University of Newcastle upon Tyne. His main publications include *The Closed Shop* (Gower, 1982, co-author), *Profit*

Sharing and Profitability (Kogan Page, 1987, co-author), and *Taming the Trade Unions* (Macmillan, 1991). He is author and co-author of numerous journal articles on employment relations. He co-authored the *Employment Policy* Report of the Adam Smith Institute (1983) and 'Measuring Inflation', an article in the *New Palgrave Dictionary of Money and Finance* (Macmillan, 1992). For the IEA he has contributed to *Trade Unions: A Century of Privilege?* (Occasional Paper 38, 1973), *The Long Debate on Poverty* (IEA Readings No.9, 1972, 2nd Edn. 1974), *Trade Unions: Public Goods or Public 'Bads'?* (IEA Readings No. 17, 1978), and he wrote a postscript to the second edition of F.A. Hayek's *1980s Unemployment and the Unions* (Hobart Paper 87, 1984). He is co-author of *Striking out Strikes* (Hobart Paper 110, 1988).

George Yarrow is Fellow and Tutor in Economics, Hertford College, Oxford, and Director of the Regulatory Policy Institute. His main academic interests are in the theory of the firm, industrial organisation, and privatisation. His main publications include (with J. Vickers) *Privatization – An Economic Analysis* (1988) and (with Helen Lawton Smith) *Social Security and Friendly Societies: Options for the Future* (1993). He contributed a chapter, 'Does Ownership Matter?', to *Privatisation & Competition: A Market Prospectus* (IEA Hobart Paperback No.28, 1989).

Dennis O'Keeffe is Senior Lecturer in the Sociology of Education and head of the Truancy Unit, University of North London. His main academic interests are the economics, sociology and political science of education. His principal recent publication is *Truancy in Modern Secondary Schools*, Her Majesty's Stationery Office, 1993.

Nigel Ashford is Principal Lecturer in Politics at the University of Staffordshire. His main research interest is in the rôle of ideology as a determinant of public policy, with particular reference to the politics of the European Union, the USA and the UK. He is co-editor with Grant Jordan of *Public Policy and the Impact of the New Right*, London: Pinter, 1993.

A QUALIFIED DEFENCE

P.M. Jackson

University of Leicester

THE BRITISH WELFARE STATE is one of the triumphs of modern civilisation. Based upon the fundamental values of public service and community, it has contributed considerably to the mitigation of the worst consequences of poverty over the post-war period. Despite these tremendous achievements it faces a number of difficulties and challenges which it must successfully solve if it is to survive well into the next century.

These challenges come from a variety of sources and include:

- intellectual movements which believe that market solutions are superior to state solutions in providing for welfare;

- demographic pressures;

- a financing crisis; and

- the disincentive effects which the welfare system imposes on the rest of the economy.

In a recent review of *The State of Welfare* by Hills *et al.*[1] I concluded:

> 'the welfare state has weathered the economic storms of the past fifteen years and it has survived the ideological attacks of the 1980s. Without the welfare state the plight of many would have been unthinkable.'[2]

---

[1] J. Hills *et al.*, *The State of Welfare: The Welfare State in Britain Since 1974*, Oxford: Clarendon Press, 1990.

[2] P.M. Jackson, 'Review of Hills *et al.*', *Economic Journal*, Vol. 102, No. 410, 1992, pp.175-76.

I now defend that conclusion by exploring the problems associated with its alternatives.

The term 'welfare state' covers social security systems, transfer payments and subsidies along with the financing and provision of public services such as health, education and personal social services. The objective is to ensure that standards of living for the members of a community do not fall below a minimum level generally regarded as tolerable. Such a system insures against uncertainties such as unemployment, sickness and the infirmities of old age. How efficiently and compassionately a community deals with these issues is an indicator of its civilisation. The activities of the welfare state are, therefore, (a) income smoothing over the life cycle: resources are transferred across time from high income periods to low income periods (hence retirement pensions); (b) insurance against particular contingencies such as short periods of sickness, invalidity and unemployment; and (c) relief of poverty as when invalidity and sickness become the norm.

These ideas are incorporated in Briggs's 1961 essay on the welfare state. The welfare state's rôle is

'to modify the play of market forces in at least two directions – first by guaranteeing individuals and families a minimum income...second, by narrowing the extent of insecurity by enabling individuals and families to meet certain social contingencies (for example, sickness, old age, and unemployment) which lead otherwise to individual and family crises; and third by ensuring that all citizens without distinction of status or class are offered the best standards in relation to a certain agreed range of social services.'[3]

Expansion Beyond Beveridge

When Beveridge set down the basis of the welfare state in his report of December 1942, his ideas were significantly different from those implemented in later years. Beveridge proposed a fixed level of National Insurance contributions to be split between employers and employees. Clearly these payments would have been regressive; they would have represented a higher proportion for those on lower incomes. Also, he proposed that National Insurance contributions

---

[3] A. Briggs, 'The Welfare State in Historical Perspective', *Archíves Europeannes de Sociologic*, Vol.2, 1961, pp. 221-59, quotation cited from p.222.

would pay for National Insurance benefits. The system he had in mind was based upon insurance principles with the state acting as insurer of last resort. Any redistribution of income which might come about was to be effected via the Exchequer supplement which was 20 per cent of the total fund. Beveridge envisaged a much restricted scheme compared to that which was realised. Moreover, he thought it would take about 20 years to introduce the scheme, with the exception of pensions which were to be given immediately to all existing pensioners. Whilst he regarded the National Insurance scheme as one of last resort which would diminish in significance as economic growth improved, the reverse has been the outcome. The welfare state has expanded as real incomes have grown and more and more people have become dependent upon state provision of certain services. This suggests that the distribution of real income gains has been uneven and/or that growing real incomes have enabled the welfare state to move into new areas not envisaged by Beveridge.

Why is this? Welfare benefits have been related to economic growth and have increased in line with real incomes in the economy. Entitlements to benefits have expanded. The original regressive flat-rate contributions have been replaced by progressive contributions; for example, the 1959 Boyd-Carpenter Plan of graduated pensions developed into earnings-related pensions and earnings-related contributions. This principle was extended to other earnings-related benefits.

About 30 per cent of total public spending in the UK is devoted to the social security budget. Of this 48 per cent is allocated to pensions; another significant element is child benefit. The UK welfare state faces pressures from population growth and the changing composition of the population; 16 per cent were over 64 years of age in 1991. This will rise to 25 per cent by 2041. The State Earnings Related Pension Scheme (SERPS) cost £1 billion in 1990/91. By the year 2040 it will rise to £16 billion at 1990/91 prices. As more and more people become eligible for the basic pension it would add 11 per cent to basic pension costs over the next 50 years, or 0·6 per cent of GDP.

Old-age pensions and child benefit are universal benefits and are paid irrespective of an individual's means. In 1979 the elderly were 26 per cent of the poorest tenth of the population. By 1987 this figure had dropped to 12 per cent. Indeed, 1 in 20 pensioners are in the top 20 per cent of household incomes and 1 in 8 are in the top 40 per cent. Their incomes in old age come from savings, including occupational pensions – 60 per cent of men currently retiring have an occupational pension.

At the bottom end 1·4 million pensioners need their pension topped up from income support; 2·0 million pensioners qualify for housing benefit to assist them with their rents and 3·0 million receive assistance with Council Tax payments.

What this implies is a reconsideration of the desirability of state pensions as universal benefits. Pensions could be better targeted especially on people in most need, that is, pensioners over 75 years of age.

Similar arguments apply to the universal child benefit. One in six families is in the top 20 per cent of household incomes whilst two in five families are in the top 40 per cent. Many of them do not need it. For the poorest 20 per cent of two-parent, two-children families, child benefit represents 8 per cent of family net income! It is even larger for many lone-parent families.

Whilst the real incomes of people in employment rose significantly during the 1980s the real incomes of the poorest 20 per cent of the population (that is, the long-term unemployed; elderly pensioners and lone-parent families) fell by £160 a year on average.

Pressures of Social Change

Significant social changes have placed more pressures on the welfare state. The numbers in long-term unemployment (over six months) have increased; the extended family has broken down; and the number of lone-parent families has increased. A more flexible labour market has increased the propensity of firms to lay workers off during the down-turn of the business cycle whilst low-paid part-time jobs, even for males, have replaced full-time jobs. The social landscape is significantly different from the days of the Beveridge Report.

The British system of welfare payments is 'universal' – that is, it guarantees to everyone a minimum income without a means test. Universal systems are expensive and tend to return income to the middle classes rather than to people in most need. This is what Buchanan referred to as the 'churning' welfare state.[4] There is today a demand amongst OECD countries to move away from expensive universal social welfare systems and towards means-tested, poverty-alleviating benefits, targeting benefits on the most needy. Those who advocate this system might wish to consider Australia as a case study.

---

[4] J. M. Buchanan, *The Political Economy of the Welfare State*, Stockholm: Industrial Institute for Economic and Social Research, 1988.

Australia's welfare system is not universalist, but selectivist. There is more relative poverty within Australian society compared to other OECD countries.

Targeting benefits on people in most need, whilst attractive in principle, has many practical problems which should not be ignored. Benefits can be differentiated and there is a much richer range of policy choices than is often supposed. This is evident if family benefits are compared across different countries in Western Europe and North America. Implementing targeting schemes is, however, difficult and expensive because information about the claimants' circumstances is imperfect and has to be monitored and checked.

'Insiders' and 'Outsiders'

It is frequently claimed that the welfare state reduces personal freedoms. So it does, but so also does poverty caused by factors outside the individual's control. Individuals do not as a rule voluntarily enter into a state of poverty. Ill-health, disability, and other constraints prevent them from gaining access to the labour market. They become 'outsiders', and the longer they are outsiders the longer they are likely to remain outsiders.

The human condition of the outsider is not to be envied. Few wish to be outside; they are not voluntarily enjoying leisure whilst others work. Their earnest objective is to become insiders – but how? This is one of the challenges of the age. If the pressures on the welfare state are to be eased it is necessary to confront the barriers between insiders and outsiders with a view to breaking them down. In so doing, both negative and positive freedoms would be created. In the meantime the welfare state ensures the creation of positive freedoms for the outsiders whilst threatening the negative freedoms of insiders. This is a fine balancing act as Buchanan has demonstrated in his *Limits of Liberty : Between Anarchy and Leviathan*.[5]

Much attention has been given to the disincentive effects created by raising taxation to fund the welfare state. The argument is that work incentives, job search and saving and risk-taking incentives are diminished with the result that the productive potential of the economy is constrained and growth in real incomes is reduced. Whilst such

---

[5] J.M. Buchanan, *Limits of Liberty: Between Anarchy and Leviathan*, Chicago: Chicago University Press, 1975. Also A. Lindbeck, 'Individual Freedom and Welfare State Policy', *European Economic Review*, Vol. 32, March 1988.

disincentives exist in principle, empirical studies have either failed to find them or have shown them to be small and of little consequence.[6]

Is the private sector a reasonable alternative provider of welfare services? Income smoothing requires individuals to be able to borrow whilst the relief of poverty at some point in the future requires the availability of insurance. Would private capital markets and insurance companies provide the means of achieving the objectives currently performed by the welfare state? There is every reason to conclude that these are not perfect substitutes.

Difficulties in Private Services

Some of the problems involved in transferring welfare provision to the private sector can be illustrated from insurance companies. They face two severe problems, which reduce the efficiency of the insurance concept: adverse selection and moral hazard. Adverse selection arises when bad risks become over-represented in the portfolio of an insurance company. It increases premiums, with the consequence that low-risk individuals will leave the scheme unless different classes of risks are charged different rates. The task is to identify different risk classes. Past behaviour is not necessarily a good predictor of risks. Consider, for example, if someone was to insure against unemployment in the future. Which current forms of employment would be regarded as good risks? A few years ago people employed in private financial services or the government might have been regarded as good risks, but not now.

It is instructive to note that Winston Churchill, when engaged in the House of Commons debate on the introduction of National Insurance in 1911, used an 'adverse selection' argument:

> 'Voluntary schemes of unemployment insurance...have always failed because those men likely to be unemployed resorted to them, and, consequently, there is a preponderance of bad risks...which must be fatal to the success of the scheme.'[7]

Moral hazard arises because being insured is likely to affect behaviour. For example, if someone is insured against unemployment

---

[6] C.V. Brown, *Taxation and the Incentive to Work*, Oxford: Oxford University Press, 1980; C V. Brown and C. Sandford, 'Taxation and Incentives', in C. Sandford (ed.), *Key Issues in Tax Reform*, Bath: Fiscal Publications, 1993.

[7] *Hansard*, 1911, Vol. 26, col. 495.

and then becomes unemployed the incentive to find another job is blunted. Or sickness may be faked in the case of health insurance. Private insurance, therefore, does not automatically solve the problems often thought to be particular to social insurance schemes. Adverse selection and moral hazard add to the cost of the insurance and premiums will rise. Alternatively, complex and expensive monitoring and administrative control procedures would need to be introduced; but again the costs of insurance would rise.

Many risks simply cannot be insured against under a private scheme or insured at a price that can be afforded. People who become long-term outsiders are uninsurable, whilst those who become sick will face higher premiums in the future. Profit-maximising private insurance companies will be interested only in low risks or in people with high risks who are able and willing to pay ('cream skimming'). Whilst private insurance might be an alternative for old-age pension provision for people in stable lifetime employment, it fails for those whose employment experience is regularly punctuated by long spells of involuntary unemployment or for the chronically sick and infirm. Private insurance for unemployment and sickness contingencies simply fails to exist on a scale required to provide minimum incomes for those in most need.

Entitlements are defined within a standard contract. The definition of entitlements for all possible contingencies would simply be too complex and expensive under private insurance. Because the private sector has the incentive to satisfy the profit motive it would tend to minimise payments made to insured people. There will, therefore, be a stronger tendency for the insured to be in contest with the scheme over the interpretation of the small print. This will not only delay payments but also involve both parties in bargaining costs and hassle. Government schemes can be more lenient in their interpretation of the match between entitlements and contingencies. They have discretion to vary entitlements with needs.

Insurance companies also face severe 'agency' problems. This is clearly demonstrated in the American system of health care insurance. Health care costs in America have risen rapidly as hospitals pass on large rents to insurance companies which in turn recover their costs from increased premiums. The transactions and monitoring costs of controlling hospital and other health care costs are large. Agency problems, of course, also exist under a system of state provision, but to assume that privatisation will eliminate or minimise these problems is too strong.

7

Finally, people who purchase insurance face considerable uncertainties: the probability of the insurable event occurring; the real value of the payout; what happens if premiums are not kept up; the surrender value of the policy. Individuals are not well informed, and it is easy to fool them, especially in complex matters such as pensions and insurance. The problems of Robert Maxwell and the Mirror Group pensioners all too readily illustrate this criticism. Also, when individuals are in most need they are often at their most vulnerable.

Future Viability: A Re-Assessment of State Welfare

The logic which supports the argument for the failure and imperfection of insurance markets is well established.[8] Indeed, the origin of the insurance problem is to be found in the imperfection of capital markets. 'What makes unemployment so painful...is not the loss in lifetime income, but the inability of individuals to borrow to meet current needs. Thus, the true problem of capital markets'.[9] Similar arguments are provided by Diamond[10] and Fleming.[11]

The demographic and social problems that are placing pressures on the welfare state do, however, need to be put into perspective. Over the next 50 years they will (if unchecked) claim about 4 per cent of GDP – the recession over the past three years claimed 5 per cent through increased unemployment benefits, and so on. Unemployment benefits have crowded out many other forms of state spending. The future viability of the welfare state will depend upon a review of the entitlements to welfare, a reassessment of universality, success in economic recovery and the reduction of unemployment.

Private provision of income smoothing and insurance against certain contingencies offer some scope as substitutes for elements of welfare spending currently provided by the state. The scope, however, is limited and brings with it the three problems of adverse selection, moral hazard and agency. Nor does it necessarily protect the recipients of the services from the monopoly power of professional groups.

---

[8] A.B. Atkinson, 'Social Insurance', Ch. 11 in A. B. Atkinson, *Incomes and the Welfare State*, Cambridge: Cambridge University Press, 1995.

[9] J.E. Stiglitz, *The Economic Role of the State*, Oxford: Basil Blackwell, 1989, p.65.

[10] P.A. Diamond, 'A framework for social security analysis', *Journal of Public Economics*, Vol. 8, 1977, pp.275-98.

[11] J.S.Flemming, 'Aspects of optimal unemployment insurance: search, leisure and savings and capital market imperfections', *Journal of Public Economics*, Vol. 10, 1978, pp. 403-25.

Without the welfare state the plight of many people would have been unthinkable. Whilst voluntary societies and charities would have assisted the long-term unemployed, the infirm and the chronically sick, collective social insurance has made their lives very much better. Anyone who cares to dispute this proposition should visit those societies which have no such system.

2

EDUCATION WITHOUT THE STATE

Edwin G. West
Carleton University, Ottawa

To CONJECTURE A BRITAIN that had never experienced government intervention in education is not without problems. It would be helpful, for instance, if we could point to the experience of another country similar in all respects but without 'free' and compulsory state education. Yet this is hardly possible because government intervention prevails throughout Western countries and seems to be the inevitable consequence of the growth of political democracy.

The historical attachment to democracy is sometimes explained as the need to protect the poor. But since democracy is a simple *majority* voting institution, how can we expect the poor, who constitute a *minority*, to be particularly well served?

Pressure Groups, Politicians, Bureaucratic Self-Interest

More sophisticated observers in the economic school of public choice are now viewing democracy as an institution operated largely by special interest groups, vote-maximising politicians and self-seeking bureaucracies, which do not represent the poor. Many scholars now conclude that the eventual dominant objective of government school systems is not to promote the greatest happiness of parents or children, or the most efficient schooling, but to transfer wealth to educators. In line with this view, education illustrates, indeed, one of the most glaring examples of rent-seeking – the extraction of privileges from government – that the world has ever seen.

If the government school system is so firmly attached to politics, is it not merely academic to imagine Britain without its state education whilst continuing with its democracy? There are at least three possible responses.

- *First,* because democracy can appear in several varieties, it would be enlightening to conjecture the differences in education that could result from variations in constitutional rules and structures. They would include more inclusive voting rules (reinforced as distinct from simple majority voting), decentralisation as opposed to central government dominance, restrictions and/or extensions of the franchise, and increased use of referenda.

- *Second,* even if it now seems impossible to return to a world of almost negligible state involvement in education, it is still a useful undertaking to correct public misunderstanding about schooling before the famous Forster Act of 1870 which introduced government schools.

- *Third,* since the present extent of rent-seeking depends on differences in the volume of information about education possessed (a) by the suppliers (teachers and officials) and (b) by the voters at large, the equilibrium could eventually change, at least at the margin, as parents, families and members of the general public became more informed. This essay will focus on the second and the third of these possibilities.

An Extension of the pre-1870 Trends Without the 1870 Act

Henry Brougham's Select Committee reported (in 1820) that in 1818 about one in 17 of the total population of England and Wales was being schooled and paid for largely by working parents. If education is a 'normal' economic good, we would expect this measure of schooling to increase with the rise in incomes. Brougham's Committee reported that the figures for 1818 were a considerable improvement on 1800 when the earliest estimate was made. Ten years later, in 1828, Brougham in his private capacity followed up the report for 1818 with a 5 per cent sample survey of his own, using the same sources (the parochial clergy) as before. His findings suggested that the number of children in schools had doubled.

Such evidence alone would challenge the view that the desire for education has to be *imposed* by the state. If education 'consumption' begins to appear and to rise with income, the most appropriate government strategy might be one or more of the following:

TABLE 1:
Growth in Private Schooling, England and Wales, 1818-1858

Year	Population	Average Annual Growth Rate of Population (%)	Number of Day Scholars	Average Annual Growth Rate of Day Scholars (%)
1818	11,642,683	1·40	674,883	3·60
1833	14,386,415	1·47	1,276,947	3·16
1851	17,927,609	1·47	2,144,378	3·16
1858	19,523,103	1·21	2,525,462	2·35

Source: The 1851 Census and the 1861 Newcastle Commission.

- redistribution of income to enable more parents to pay;

- more patience at a time of steady income growth; and

- concentration on removal of barriers to such growth.

The rising income correlation with the growth in education suggests that, as income per head increased in the 19th century, schooling grew 'vigorously' in response. Whereas the actual growth of income per head in the years 1801-71 was slightly over 1 per cent per annum, the average annual growth rate of day scholars was well over 2 per cent (last column of Table 1). The growth of schooling in England and Wales during this period, it should be emphasised, came before it was made free, compulsory and supplied by government.

The annual growth of scholars also exceeded the annual growth of population (columns 3 and 5 of Table 1). During the compilation of the 1851 educational census, it was reported that the average duration of attendance at school of working-class children was nearly five years. The Newcastle Commission reported that by 1858 (seven years later), it had risen to nearly six years. And the attainment of an education threshold for most people was reported in the 1861 Commission's conclusion that '*almost everyone receives some amount of schooling at some period or another*'.

It is true that government subsidies to schools were introduced in 1833, but their aggregate value was very low (only £20,000 in 1833). By 1841, they were still so small that they were considerably less than the private school fee revenue collected from parents in the City of

13

Bristol alone. The major 19th-century legislation came in 1870 with the Forster Act. Yet by 1869 *most* people in England and Wales were literate, *most* children were receiving a schooling and *most* parents, working class included, were paying fees for it.[1]

It is surely reasonable to suggest that since *per capita* income continued to grow after 1858, both the number of day scholars and the average years of school attendance would have continued to grow. Since, moreover, there would have been no crowding out of private by government schools, the private sector would have continued to be diverse, with denominational church schools playing a much stronger rôle than after the Forster Act.

Comparisons with Developing Countries in the Late 20th Century

By all standard measures used today, Britain was an under-developed country right down to the later part of the 19th century. In the light of this it is relevant, in retrospect, to compare three prominent findings concerning developing countries today. They are as follows:

- The growth of education combats the Malthusian spectre of over-population – that the population would grow (geometrically) faster than production (arithmetically).

- Education growth leads to increases in *per capita* incomes which, in turn, improve health and lower mortality; and since these improvements enhance the pay-off to human capital investment, the growth in education becomes cumulative or, at least, self-enforcing.

- As *per capita* incomes increase, parents voluntarily spend more on education.

These findings pertain to the systematic study of the records of over 100 developing countries since 1960.[2]

Consider now the presently developed countries England and Wales in their developing years.[3] With a population of nearly 12 million in

---

[1] Edwin G. West, *Education and the State*, London: Institute of Economic Affairs, 1965; 2nd edn., 1970, p.xvii; 3rd edn. (revised and extended), Indianapolis, IN: Liberty Fund, 1994.

[2] Gary S. Becker, 'Human Capital and Poverty Alleviation', HRO Working Paper, World Bank, March 1995.

[3] The historical details that follow are in West (1994), *op.cit.*

1818, and no 'public' (government) schools, about one in 17 were attending private schools paid for largely by working parents. There were then no government subsidies to private schools and no laws for compulsory schooling. By 1858 the proportion of the population found in fee-paid schools had increased dramatically (almost doubled) to approximately one in eight. And by this time the percentage annual growth rate of population had fallen to 1·21 from 1·40 in 1818 (Table 1). This relationship between population and production (measured by incomes and fee-paying) is consistent with the first of the three 'modern' findings concerning the 20th-century developing countries reported above: the growth of education combats the threat of over-population. And at that time it was education without the state.

Next, we have seen that the annual growth of *per capita* income in the years 1801-71 was just over 1 per cent while the annual average growth rate of day scholars was well over 2 per cent. This combination of circumstances is consistent with the second of the three findings from 20th-century developing countries: education growth is associated with, or leads to, increases in *per capita* incomes. Moreover, it is pertinent that in Britain the years 1801-71 witnessed a drop in mortality rates, a factor that increased the yield from human capital investment.

Finally, since in Britain's case it was education largely without the state, and especially without laws of compulsory education, we have the strongest possible support for the third finding from today's developing countries: parents voluntarily spend more (directly from their own pockets) on education as their incomes rise. Indeed, the 19th-century figures for England and Wales show that the income elasticity of demand was particularly high: the desire for private education rose much faster than incomes.

The Savings in the Costs of Taxation

After 1870 direct spending on education by individual families was increasingly replaced by indirect spending for them via government. To accomplish this feat government needed enlarged tax revenues. By the 1990s the sources of taxation for state schooling have reached a record and the total revenue required is unprecedented.

At this point we have to focus on one of the major economic consequences of the collectivisation of schooling, well understood by economists but usually neglected by educationists and laymen partly because it seems excessively theoretical. The economic concept of the deadweight welfare cost of taxation arises because, instead of a

15

'perfect' tax system that uses lump-sum taxes for all revenue purposes, we impose a variety of taxes each of which causes distortions in consumption and/or resource allocation. Income taxes, for instance, cause distortions in the choices between leisure and work, excise taxes cause 'artificial' contractions of consumption of the taxed goods, and so on.

An example outlines the main issues. Suppose an excise tax is levied on television receivers thus causing an increase in price, but so high that the output falls to zero. No tax revenue is collected, and there is no direct cost of taxation (no withdrawal of private sector resources). But clearly there is another burden. Too few television sets are produced and too many other commodities. There is a misallocation of resources. We know that, without the tax, consumers had a preference for a certain quantity of television receivers and a smaller quantity of other goods. After the tax they are constrained to distort their purchases into a less preferred pattern. Consumers are obviously worse off with the resource allocation caused by the tax. This burden, or 'deadweight welfare cost', exists even though there is no direct cost of revenue collection from the tax. This example shows that, although the two types of burdens are descriptively different, they are both costs in the economist's sense. In the more typical situation, an excise tax is not so high as to reduce production to zero (and some tax revenue is raised). In this case, the two burdens of tax, the direct cost and the deadweight welfare cost, co-exist.

It is important to realise that the deadweight cost of taxation increases exponentially with increases in the share of the GNP taken by government.[4] Since this share is larger in Britain than in the USA, the calculations of deadweight cost magnitudes are even higher for Britain.

Usher[5] demonstrates that the conventional deadweight loss analysis adopted by US writers[6] underestimates the cost of raising government revenue because it ignores the welfare cost of tax evasion. This cost also increases exponentially with the share of GNP taken by government. Incorporating tax evasion costs, Usher calculates that,

---

[4] E.K. and J.M. Browning, *Public Finance and the Price System*, New York: Macmillan, 3rd edn., 1987, for instance, assume that the cost grows by roughly the square of the increase in the size of the government's share of GNP.

[5] Dan Usher, 'Tax Evasion and the Marginal Cost of Public Funds', *Economic Inquiry*, Vol. XXIV, No. 4, 1986, pp.563-86.

[6] For example, C.L. Ballard, J.B. Shoven, and J. Whalley, 'General Equilibrium Computations on the Marginal Welfare Costs of Taxation', *American Economic Review*, Vol. 75, No. 1, 1985.

with a government share of GNP of 50 per cent and tax evasion of 10 per cent, it costs 80 pence to raise £1 of extra tax revenue. In other words, the total burden on taxpayers when one extra pound of revenue is raised amounts to £1·80.

Judging from the recent economic literature as a whole, it seems reasonable to conclude that the deadweight costs of the taxes used to supply revenues for British state education in the 1990s amount to *at least* 50 per cent of the direct costs of that education. Assuming there had been no Forster Act, therefore, citizens in the late 19th century would have been spared these excessive costs. But the main significance of this examination of the tax cost applies to the present time when the share of British government in GNP is around an all-time high and the deadweight costs have increased dramatically. Thus if, starting with the year 1870, government had not intervened in the expansion of schooling, it is probable today (in 1996) that we would be spared the unprecedented excess costs in taxation for financing state education.

In British private education before 1870, the record of educational outputs such as literacy was even more impressive than the numbers of children in school and presents an even more serious problem to typical authors of social histories. Professor Mark Blaug has observed that 'Conventional histories of education neatly dispose of the problem by simply ignoring the literacy evidence'.[7] He emphasises that, since it is common in developing countries for literacy to run ahead of the numbers in school, we have to recognise the existence of numerous educational agencies outside formal state schooling (column 4 in Table 1).

These agencies in the 19th century included the adult education movement, the mutual improvement societies, the Literary and Philosophical Institutes, the Mechanics' Institutes and the Owenite Halls of Science. Professor Blaug also refers to freelance lecturers who travelled the towns and stimulated self-study among the poor. And in part-time formal education the Sunday Schools and adult evening schools were obvious examples. Simultaneously also, there were the factory schools 'which proliferated in the northern textile industry long before the 1833 Act made them mandatory'.[8]

---

[7] Mark Blaug, 'The Economics of Education in English Classical Political Economy: A Re-Examination', in A. Skinner and T. Wilson, *Essays on Adam Smith*, Oxford: Clarendon Press, 1975, p.595.

[8] Blaug, *ibid.*, p.597.

From this impressive collection of agencies outside the formal state education system, paid by parents, grandparents, employers, charities and other private sources, it is clear that they would have continued and probably strengthened had there been no Forster Act in 1870.

Non-Profit Institutions

The government schools that were introduced after 1870 were non-profit institutions and they came eventually to enjoy strong monopoly powers. One of the serious weaknesses of non-profit organisations is their sluggish response to dynamic change. Suppose, for instance, new cost-saving (or output-increasing) methods become available that have not been widely adopted so far. In a for-profit free-market system, entrepreneurs will incorporate the new methods and will seize the corresponding opportunities for entry stimulated by direct and clear income-gaining incentives. In a world of non-profit organisations, in contrast, such incentives do not exist. There are no conventional entrepreneurs, only administrators. Prompt and widespread entry by innovators is therefore not to be expected.

But does the problem apply also to the private schools many, if not most, of which are also non-profit institutions? The efficiency obstacles here are not so serious. Managers of a non-profit private school are normally sensitive to the vital contribution of donations to their budget (and therefore their personal incomes), as a direct function of the school's reputation. In addition, private school fees make a decisive difference. When a parent withdraws a child, the fee income automatically decreases and places immediate pressure on management. Government school headmasters, in contrast, have no such direct economic pressure from their parent-customers.

Even though most of the private schools might have remained non-profit organisations after 1870 without the Forster Act, they would have been subject to increasing competition from the vast array of the non-formal private education agencies. This competition would have been strengthened in the absence of compulsion for there would have continued to be a legal right to quit formal education and to seek the competing informal private alternatives at any time. The effect of compulsion has usually been to strengthen the monopoly power of the government school, especially when, as happened in the late 19th century, the average family's income was pre-empted through indirect (regressive) taxes on goods and services to finance the so-called 'free' schooling available only in state schools.

Conclusion

The fluid, flexible, heterogeneous and competitive educational scenario of the pre-1870s is the environment that the more radical reformers of education are now demanding in many countries. The choice of *school* movement, it is maintained, has been to a large extent misinformed. What is needed is choice in *education*.

> 'School choice has not and will not lead to more productive education because the obsolete technology called "school" is inherently *inelastic*... As long as "school" refers to the traditional structure of buildings and grounds with services delivered in boxes called classrooms to which customers must be transported by car or bus, "school choice" will be unable to meaningfully alter the quality or efficiency of education.'[9]

Although this argument is perhaps extreme, it contains a substantial truth. Genuinely free markets are unpredictable in their unfolding school organisations as well as in their offerings of completely new curricula with which they constantly surprise us. The post-1870 era without the Forster Act provided precisely the setting necessary for the emergence of a truly dynamic and innovative *education* market in the 1990s.

It is unfortunate that this market was destroyed by the combined action of politicians, bureaucrats and rent-seekers, action that not only reduced the potential quality of education but also imposed on citizens enormous financial burdens, especially in the deadweight costs of taxation.

---

[9] Lewis Perleman, *School's Out*, New York: Avon Books, 1992, pp.186-87.

3

MEDICAL CARE WITHOUT THE STATE

David G. Green
Director,
IEA Health and Welfare Unit

THE TURNING POINTS in the suppression of spontaneous medical provision came in 1911 and 1948. In 1911 primary medical care was effectively nationalised for employees, but it was not until 1948 that hospitals were compulsorily brought within the embrace of the government. If the state had not effectively nationalised primary medical care in 1911 and if it had refrained from nationalising the hospitals in 1948, how might medical services have developed? Plainly, absolute reliance should not be placed on any prediction, but we can draw reasonable inferences from the rate and nature of change in primary medical care before 1911 and hospital provision up to 1948.

Primary Medical Care

In Britain, primary medical care was provided in a variety of ways at the turn of the century. The very poor relied on the poor law. Provision for the rest of the population fell into three main categories. *First*, many sought medical care as private patients and paid a fee to the doctor of their choice. Fees varied according to income. *Second*, a large section of the population obtained care free of charge through charities. Particularly in London and the larger towns, some people used the outpatient departments of the voluntary hospitals; others used free dispensaries where they existed. *Third*, and most common, were pre-payment schemes, usually called contract practice, based on the payment of a fixed annual capitation fee.

Private Fees

The majority of the Royal Commission on the Poor Laws of 1909 found that 'many', including those from the 'poorest working class', paid fees as private patients in preference to joining clubs.[1] It had been told by the medical officer of health in Manchester that a 'very considerable' number of persons earning less than 30 shillings a week paid ordinary fees.[2] And there is evidence that this had been so for many years. Fifty years earlier the *Association Medical Journal* said in 1853 that 'many' workers earning only 12s to 15s a week paid the customary private fee.[3] This is not as surprising as it may seem, for doctors charged fees according to income, and the lowest fee was within the grasp of the low-paid worker. Rent was usually taken as a rough indicator of means. An official tariff in *Whitaker's Almanack* for 1900 distinguished three scales: rents from £10 to £25 a year; £25 to £50; and £50 to £100 plus. The minimum fee for a surgery consultation for the poorest class was 2s 6d.[4] Such fees, as long as they had to be paid only occasionally, were within the means of most wage earners. In 1906 the average wage of unskilled workers was about 22s a week; for the semi-skilled, about 28s; and for the skilled worker, around 37s a week.[5]

Free Care

Many poor people sought care from the voluntary hospitals and charitable dispensaries, which provided advice and medicine free to those on low incomes. These were available in most large towns. The system at the Newcastle free dispensary was that patients with a subscriber's letter of recommendation received attendance and medicine free, whilst 'casuals' paid 2d for medicine prescribed.[6]

Of greatest importance for the supply of free medical care were the outpatient departments of the voluntary hospitals. Using figures

---

[1] Royal Commission on the Poor Laws and Relief of Distress, *Report*, London: HMSO, 1909, p.259.

[2] *Ibid.*, Appendix IV, Q. 38390.

[3] *Association Medical Journal*, 22 July 1853, p.652.

[4] *Whitaker's Almanack*, 1900, p.411; R.M.S. McConaghey, 'Medical practice in the days of Mackenzie' (The James Mackenzie Memorial Lecture), *The Practitioner*, Vol. 196 (1966), p.155; M.J. Peterson, *The Medical Profession in Mid-Victorian London*, Berkeley: University of California Press, 1978, pp.211-13.

[5] G. Routh, *Occupation and Pay in Great Britain 1906-79*, 2nd edn., London: Macmillan, 1980, pp.100, 106, 113.

[6] Royal Commission on the Poor Laws and Relief of Distress, *Report*, London: HMSO, 1909, Appendix V, Q. 50566.

published by the Hospital Sunday Fund, Arthur (later Sir Arthur) Newsholme estimated the proportion of the metropolitan population obtaining free medical care in 1907 at one in four.[7] Outpatient departments were important in the great majority of large towns, but the London figures are not typical of the country as a whole because of the heavy concentration of hospitals in the capital. Provincial figures varied. In Newcastle in 1894 the figure was one in two, in Edinburgh one in three, in Glasgow one in five, in Cardiff one in seven, and in Portsmouth one in 14.[8]

Contract Practice

The various types of pre-payment scheme are identified in a report of the medico-political committee of the British Medical Association (BMA), published in 1905.[9] Each type of contract practice was based on the principle of the flat-rate annual contribution, usually payable quarterly, entitling the contributor to any number of consultations during the period covered. Some such clubs were based at factories, others were organised by charities; some were run on commercial lines, some by individual doctors, some by local associations of doctors, and some by the friendly societies. By far the most important numerically were the friendly society schemes.

A number of doctors were employed by *works clubs*. Workers at a factory or mine arranged with their employer to deduct an agreed sum from their pay for the provision of medical attendance and medicines for themselves, and usually for their families. Some doctors were paid a fixed salary, others an annual amount per patient. The most resilient of the works clubs were the 'medical aid societies' founded by the miners and steelworkers of the Welsh valleys.

The *provident dispensaries* were semi-charities, funded partly by the contributions of beneficiaries and partly by the charitable donations of the honorary members. These self-supporting dispensaries were often founded as alternatives to the free dispensaries, many of which had been established during the 18th century. Free dispensaries were felt to create a permanently dependent section of the population; the provident

---

[7] *British Medical Journal*, 14 September 1907, p.658; *Lancet*, 1 June 1907, pp.1,543-50.

[8] *British Medical Journal*, 14 September 1907, p.658.

[9] British Medical Association Medico-Political Committee, 'An investigation into the economic conditions of contract medical practice in the United Kingdom', *British Medical Journal Supplement*, 22 July 1905, pp.1-96 (hereinafter, *BMJ Supplement*, 22 July 1905).

23

dispensaries, by contrast, aimed to enable the poor to make as much of a contribution as they could afford, with the balance supplied by charity.

The BMA acknowledged that many of those in provident dispensaries, private clubs, public medical services, and medical societies were 'so poor' that they were unable to pay private fees at working-class rates. In rural districts, in particular, clubs were said to provide for the 'thrifty but very poor'.[10] The Leicester Provident Dispensary, one of the strongest, had 50,798 members in 1907 and ran a small maternity home and cottage hospital. Fees were a penny a week for adults, half for children; or 3½d. a week for a man, wife and all children under 14.[11]

Some contract medical practice was organised on commercial lines by *medical aid companies*. The National Medical Aid Company, for instance, offered medical attendance as an inducement to obtain life insurance.[12]

Among the great variety of arrangements made by the *friendly societies* for the supply of medical care, three proved most popular: the lodge system, medical institutes, and approved panels.

The traditional system in the large federations was for each *lodge* to employ a single medical officer. Usually the appointment was made by a free vote of all the members present at a general meeting. Sometimes doctors were invited to submit tenders before the election. In some areas several medical officers were appointed to a branch or a combination of branches, and the members then enjoyed a free choice among the available doctors. Sometimes medical officers were appointed at the pleasure of the branch, and sometimes for a fixed period of three months, six months, or a year.

From about 1869 a movement developed to found *medical institutes* to employ full-time medical officers serving the whole family. Groups of lodges banded together, raised funds and purchased or rented premises. Organisation was under the control of a committee of delegates which appointed one or more full-time medical officers, who usually received a fixed salary plus free accommodation. The medical officers' duties usually included general medical and surgical

---

[10] *Ibid.*, p.9.

[11] Royal Commission on the Poor Laws and Relief of Distress, *Report*, London: HMSO, 1909, Appendix IV, Q. 47501.

[12] *Lancet*, 5 October 1895, p.875.

attendance. Dispensing was carried out by the medical institute's dispenser to ensure use of the highest quality drugs.

By the turn of the century the *closed panel* system was growing in popularity. Friendly society members appointed doctors to an approved list. In Leicester, for instance, since the 1870s the societies had separated medical attendance from dispensing. By 1911 they had a board of 32 doctors who would attend and prescribe for all members. Members could choose freely among them.[13]

The National Deposit Friendly Society evolved a unique system, much disliked by the BMA. Members paid flat-rate annual contributions which entitled them to claim from the society a fixed proportion (usually two-thirds or three-quarters) of doctors' fees. The fee paid by the society was 2s 6d for a home visit, inclusive of medicines, and 1s 6d per surgery consultation.[14] In 1904 the BMA's medico-political committee recommended that no such system should be allowed to develop. They opposed it because doctors serving the National Deposit Society often accepted the society's part-payment in full settlement of the account, which made it difficult for the BMA to achieve its aim of extracting the highest fee affordable by each income group.

There were also a large number of clubs organised by doctors themselves. Many of these *doctor's clubs* employed collectors to recruit new members as well as to call regularly for patients' contributions. The collector's commission was occasionally as low as 5 per cent but sometimes reached 25 per cent.[15]

Public medical services were rather like medical aid societies, but the latter were controlled by lay committees, and public medical services were 'under the entire control of the medical profession'. In 1905 public medical services were still a recent phenomenon. Usually they had been founded by the local branch of the BMA to combat provident dispensaries, medical aid societies, or friendly societies.[16]

Extent of Coverage

How many people were covered by these arrangements? Of the 12 million originally included in the National Insurance scheme of 1911,

---

[13] *Oddfellows Magazine*, July 1911, pp.353-54.

[14] *British Medical Journal*, 18 January 1896, p.172.

[15] British Medical Association Medico-Political Committee, *op. cit.*

[16] *Ibid.*, p.23.

TABLE 1:
Receipt of Poor Relief, 1849-1892, All Recipients

Year	No. of Indoor Poor*	No. per 1,000 of Population	No. of Outdoor Poor*	No. per 1,000 of Population	Total (Indoor plus outdoor)	No. per 1,000 of Population
1849	133,513	7·7	955,146	55·0	1,088,659	62·7
1852	111,323	6·2	804,352	44·7	915,675	50·9
1862	132,236	6·6	784,906	39·0	917,142	45·6
1872	149,200	6·6	828,000	36·3	977,200	42·9
1882	183,374	7·1	604,915	23·2	788,289	30·3
1892	186,607	6·4	558,150	19·2	744,757	25·6

Source: Royal Commission on the Aged Poor, 1895, *Report*, Vol. 1, p.ix.

* The indoor poor were those receiving relief in the workhouse, and the outdoor poor those receiving relief in their own homes. The proportion of the 'not able-bodied' had also fallen between 1862 and 1892.

at least 9 million were already members of self-administered mutual aid schemes.

It is difficult to arrive at a reliable estimate of the number of people dependent on charitable care. Figures have been quoted for the usage of outpatient departments of voluntary hospitals. In London the figure was perhaps 25 per cent of the population, in Newcastle upon Tyne, 50 per cent and in Portsmouth, 7 per cent. The data are not available to calculate a reliable national average, but it was probably 10 to 15 per cent. However, people using outpatient departments would not necessarily have relied wholly on their local hospital. Evidence to the Royal Commission on the Poor Laws of 1909 suggests that some also paid private fees from time to time and that some joined pre-payment schemes but were unable to keep up the contributions.

A more reliable estimate can be given for dependence on the poor law. In 1895 the Royal Commission on the Aged Poor reported on the reliance of the elderly population on poor relief. The Commission produced figures showing reliance on the poor law by the 'able-bodied' and the 'not able-bodied', a category almost wholly comprising the elderly infirm.

Table 1 shows that the total number of paupers (able-bodied and not able-bodied) as a proportion of the population had fallen between 1849 and 1892, including the proportion receiving relief outside the workhouse.

The Commission showed the number of people receiving poor relief on a single day. The total population of England and Wales in 1891 was 29 million, of which 700,746 (2·4 per cent) were receiving poor relief on 1 January 1892. The figure includes those who received medical relief only. It also reported on the number who received relief at one time or another during 1892: 1,573,074, or 5·4 per cent of the population.[17]

Thus, during the course of a year in the 1890s, about 5 per cent of the population relied on the poor law, 10-15 per cent on free care from charitable institutions, about 75 per cent on mutual aid, and the remainder paid private fees.

The Uninsured After National Health Insurance

The period from 1911 to 1948 is of particular interest because the working population was covered by the national insurance scheme but

---

[17] Royal Commission on the Aged Poor, 1895, *Report*, Vol. 1, p.xii.

wives and children were not. As a result, they found it necessary to rely largely on non-government health care services, thus allowing us to trace the evolution of the market in health care well into the modern era, and to gauge how the whole population might have fared if the state had confined its rôle to provision of a safety net rather than a public-sector monopoly.

The main types of provision continued to be: outpatient departments of the voluntary hospitals, free dispensaries, provident dispensaries, friendly society lodge practice, insurance against medical fees (including friendly society approved panels), public medical services, private doctors' clubs, works clubs, and friendly society medical institutes.

Many people continued to use outpatient departments instead of a general practitioner, even though by the 1930s many voluntary hospitals were encouraging, or even requiring, patients to go to their GP first. In 1935 the 1,103 voluntary hospitals attended 5·6 million outpatients.[18] Some public hospitals performed a similar rôle.

Free dispensaries financed by charities continued to function in many large towns. In the mid-1930s there were over 20 in the London area alone. Provident dispensaries also continued to operate. In the London area there were nearly 20. The Battersea Provident Dispensary was one of the largest with over 6,000 members in 1936.[19]

Private medical clubs continued to function, but it is impossible to estimate how many people were covered. In the judgement of the BMA survey of 1938-39 private clubs were 'gradually dying out'. In the 'great majority' of cases divisional secretaries reported that there were no private clubs, often because they had been absorbed into the BMA's public medical services. Rates tended to be a least 3d a week, although local conventions varied enormously.[20] By the late 1930s, it is unlikely that more than 100,000 persons were covered by private club membership.

Many factories and all collieries provided medical attendance. Some were managed by the employer and some by committees representing employees. Usually such schemes covered families as well as employees. There were about one million miners in the mid-1930s.

---

[18] Political and Economic Planning, *Report on the British Health Services*, London, 1937, p.231.

[19] *Ibid*, p.152.

[20] British Medical Association, General Practice Committee, Documents 1938-39, GP107, 1-6.

Their dependants must have accounted for between 2 and 2·5 million people.

The BMA had been promoting the establishment of 'public medical services'. The largest was in London, and by 1937 throughout the country there were nearly 80 services with 650,000 subscribers. A survey of 51 public medical services found that for each subscription 1·86 persons were 'at risk'. On this basis a total of about 1·2 million people were covered by public medical services.[21]

Most people covered by lodge practice before 1911 fell under national insurance, but the lodges continued to provide for the women and children who were outside the national insurance scheme. According to the BMA's 1935-36 and 1938-39 surveys of contract practice rates, contract practice for adult members of friendly societies was 'steadily diminishing'. But it was still to be found in many areas.[22]

Competition

Most notable among the organisations which offered competition and restrained medical fees were the friendly society medical institutes and the Welsh medical aid societies. In the 1930s the medical institutes had only about 150,000 voluntary members (in addition to national insurance members), but they were distributed throughout England in over 60 large towns. Only one serious competitor in a locality was required to upset BMA price-fixing, and the medical institutes consequently had an effect on prices out of all proportion to the size of their membership. This market power earned them the implacable hostility of the medical profession. As a result, when the NHS was being planned the BMA's hostility was decisive in ensuring that no rôle at all was permitted for medical institutes.

The best available evidence is contained in the BMA surveys of 1935-36 and 1938-39. They show that many rates were below national insurance capitation fees. Medical institutes, in particular, kept rates down. The Reading public medical service (run by the BMA) had the lowest fees in the whole country and had found it impossible to raise charges because of active competition from the Amalgamated Friendly Societies of Reading, a state of affairs which caused the BMA's public medical services sub-committee 'considerable anxiety'.

---

[21] *British Medical Journal Supplement*, 10 December 1938, pp.357-62.

[22] BMA, Medico-Political Committee, Documents, 1936-37, MP31, 14-18.

Combining the BMA's findings with the figures published by the Registrar of Friendly Societies allows us to estimate the number of people obtaining medical care through the friendly societies. In 1930 there were 700 juvenile friendly societies with 185,000 members covered for medical care. In addition, the adult friendly societies had 261,000 junior members in 1930, making a total of 446,000 juvenile members. Of the total adult friendly society membership of 3,506,000, the great majority of female members would have subscribed for medical care. The Registrar did not publish separate figures for male and female members, but the evidence of the National Conference of Friendly Societies to the Beveridge committee of 1942 suggests that women comprised about a quarter of total voluntary membership. In 1941, 24 per cent of the 4·6 million members were female.[23] Using this formula, of the 3·5 million adult voluntary members in 1930 around 840,000 would have been women. Most would have paid for medical benefit. Some of the male members would also have attended lodge doctors. If only 10 per cent did so, it would suggest a figure of about 280,000. All told, at least somewhere in the region of 1·5 million persons, including children who were members of the adult friendly societies as well as of special juvenile societies, must have been obtaining medical care through friendly societies (other than deposit societies) in the mid-1930s. This estimate is based on registered friendly society membership. In addition, there were probably an equal number of unregistered friendly society members.

After the 1911 Act some friendly societies developed new schemes for insurance against doctors' fees. Some medical schemes provided for repayment of the whole fee, and some for part. In most cases a doctor had to be selected from a panel which had agreed to charge specified fees. Schemes run on part-payment principles (co-insurance) expanded rapidly. In 1936 over 1·3 million members of the National Deposit Friendly Society were covered for payment of a proportion of doctors' bills, as were 57,000 members of the Teachers Provident Society.[24] Until 1948, National Deposit Friendly Society members paid 2s 6d for a surgery attendance and 3s 6d for a home visit, including medicine. The society reimbursed either two-thirds or three-quarters of the fee.[25]

[*continued on p.33*]

---

[23] Public Records Office, PIN8/88.

[24] Political and Economic Planning, *Report on the British Health Services,* London, 1937, p.154.

[25] National Deposit Friendly Society, *Rules,* 1949, rules 87, 91.

TABLE 2:
Number of Hospital Beds for the Physically Ill, 1861-1938: England and Wales

Hospitals:	1861 No.	1861 %	1891 No.	1891 %	1911 No.	1911 %	1921 No.	1921 %	1938 No.	1938 %
Voluntary	14,772	19	29,520	26	43,221	22	56,550	25	87,235	33
Public	50,000	81	83,230	74	154,273	78	172,006	75	175,868	67
Total	65,000	100	112,750	100	197,494	100	225,556	100	263,103	100

Source: R. Pinker, *English Hospital Statistics 1861-1938*, London: Heinemann, 1966, pp. 49-50.

TABLE 3:
Hospital Income, 1935

Maintenance	London		Provinces		Scotland	
	£,000	per cent	£,000	per cent	£,000	per cent
Subscriptions & Donations	1,334	31	1,668	20	362	24
Contributory Schemes & Patients' Contributions	1,369	32	3,882	49	330	23
Public & Other Services	364	9	616	8	67	5
Investments	677	15	894	11	318	22
Other receipts	–	–	59	1	24	1
Extraordinary Means (Nearly all legacies)	581	13	860	11	372	25
Total available for running costs	4,325	100	7,973	100	1,473	100
Capital receipts	927	–	1,224	–	365	–

Source: PEP, 1937, p.233.

However, according to the BMA, a 'considerable number' of doctors continued to accept the National Deposit payment alone in full settlement of their bills, despite long-standing BMA criticism of the practice.[26]

In 1939 Great Britain had a population of 46·5 million. Of these, about 19 million were covered by national insurance. Outpatient departments of both voluntary and public hospitals must have served about 6 million; the charitable and provident dispensaries perhaps 300,000; the lodges 1·5 million; the medical institutes 150,000; fee-for-service insurance 2 million; public medical services 1·2 million; private doctors' clubs 100,000; and works clubs (including medical aid societies) about 3 million. According to these estimates about 14·2 million individuals would have been covered by the above schemes. It seems probable that at least another million would have been covered by unregistered friendly societies. The remaining 12 million or so would have paid private fees.

The Hospitals

As Table 2 shows, the public sector in the form of local authorities provided over 70 per cent of hospital beds for the physically ill in the 1930s. Most of these beds were for patients suffering from infectious diseases or who required long-term accommodation due to chronic illness. The voluntary hospitals, however, provided the backbone of the acute hospital service. Nearly 60 per cent of patients (1,101,061 out of 1,882,998) requiring acute care were admitted to voluntary hospitals in 1936.[27] They also provided the overwhelming majority of teaching hospitals. As Table 2 shows, voluntary sector beds for the physically ill had been increasing as a proportion of the total during the 1920s and 1930s (Table 2).

To what extent did the voluntary hospitals rely on private finance in the 1930s and how rapidly had private funding developed? The best contemporary source of information is a report by Political and Economic Planning (PEP) on *The British Health Services*, published in 1937.

Table 3 shows that income from private sources in the mid-1930s was substantial. Much has been made of the financial crisis facing hospitals

---

[26] BMA, Medico-Political Committee, Documents 1936-37, MP75.

[27] PEP, 1937, p.257.

in the inter-war years, and in 1921 the official Cave Committee was created to investigate. It recommended the foundation of the Voluntary Hospitals Commission to distribute £500,000 from tax revenues to assist rebuilding work delayed by the War. After the early 1920s, however, no further direct grants had been received when PEP reported in 1937.

The PEP report was written by socialists who wanted a state hospital service, but it found that it had to report that in 1935 the voluntary hospitals had an annual surplus income of over £1 million. The authors of the PEP report can only give grudging praise, conceding that 'despite the depression', the majority of voluntary hospitals have 'temporarily' overcome their financial difficulties.[28]

The most important development was that of hospital contributory schemes. They were organised by or for hospitals to enable people in lower-income groups to make regular contributions entitling them, without further inquiry into their means, to receive free hospital treatment for themselves and their dependants. Employees usually paid themselves, but employers sometimes contributed an additional amount. Most of the schemes were founded between 1929 and 1934, though the Hospital Fund for London predated the First World War.

Members of the British Hospitals Contributory Schemes Association had an income of £2,722,000 largely from the 2d or 3d weekly contributions of about 5,241,000 subscribers. PEP estimated that at least 10 million persons were covered, because subscriptions earned entitlements for the whole family. In addition, a 'considerable' number of schemes had not affiliated to the association and many cottage hospital schemes were too small to affiliate.[29]

Income from charitable sources had also been growing rapidly. According to PEP, income from charitable sources in London alone averaged £800,000 between 1922 and 1926; it rose to over £1 million per year between 1927 and 1930 and in the subsequent four years of depression did not fall below £960,000. In 1935 it was £956,000 and in 1936 £1,011,000.[30]

Pay beds were also developing to provide for patients who could afford to pay between 4 and 12 guineas for their treatment. St

---

[28] PEP, 1937, p.232.

[29] PEP, 1937, p.234.

[30] PEP, 1937, p.232.

Thomas's had 40 pay beds, Guys 71 and Manchester Royal Infirmary 100.[31] Commercial insurance was also evolving. PEP reported 19 schemes attached to particular hospitals and 16 covering treatment in more than one hospital.

The growth of private funding continued after the Second World War. In 1943 there were 191 hospital contributory schemes, with nearly 10 million subscribers paying £6,528,000.[32] The Hospital Savings Association, for instance, had income from contributions of £321,000 in 1929 which by 1934 had more than doubled, despite the depression. By 1936 it was £923,000, and on the eve of the NHS in 1947 it had 2,088,000 contributors who paid £1,587,000.[33]

PEP refers to the 'astonishing sums' collected weekly from British wage earners for insurance against common risks.[34] It noted that many working-class families contributed from 2d to 6d per week to primary care services and an additional 2d to 4d per week to hospital contributory schemes.[35] But the largest amounts were contributed to life and endowment policies. In 1935 there were about two such policies in force for every person, some 93 million policies yielding an annual income in 1935 of £64 million. These payments of between 1s and 2s per week were almost entirely made by wage earners. PEP thought that if such insurance were nationalised it would be cheaper, thus releasing more working-class spending power for other types of insurance.[36]

Trends in Hospital Provision

A careful survey of the trends in hospital provision from 1861 to 1938 has been made by Robert Pinker of the LSE.

Hospital finance had changed radically between 1891 and 1938. In 1891 charitable donations comprised 52 per cent of running costs. The proportion had fallen to 41 per cent in 1921 and to 26 per cent in 1938 (Table 4). Charitable donations were being replaced by patients' pay-

---

[31] PEP, 1937, p.239.

[32] W. Beveridge, *Voluntary Action*, London: George Allen & Unwin, 1948, p.116.

[33] G. Palliser and others, *The Charitable Work of Hospital Contributory Schemes*, London: BHCSA, 1984, p.119.

[34] PEP, 1937, p.410.

[35] PEP, 1937, p.227.

[36] PEP, 1937, pp.227-28.

TABLE 4:
Percentage Distribution of Income in Selected London and Provincial Voluntary Hospitals

Hospitals	Voluntary Gifts	Investments	Receipts For Services Rendered			Other payments	Total ordinary income
			Patients' Payments	Workmen's Contributions	Total patients' payments & workmen's contributions		
1891							
London	45	44	5	2	7	5	100
Provincial	60	25	2	9	11	4	100
Total	52	35	4	5	9	4	100
1911							
London	53	35	6	2	8	4	100
Provincial	46	23	4	22	26	3	100
Total	47	31	5	11	16	3	100
1921							
London	42	22	31	3	34	3	100
Provincial	41	14	22	21	43	2	100
Total	41	18	27	11	38	3	100
1938							
London	35	16	—	—	39	9	100
Provincial	22	11	—	—	59	8	100
Total	26	13	—	—	52	8	100

Source: R. Pinker, 1966, p. 152. (Due to rounding not all rows add up to 100 per cent.)

Note: Table shows only hospitals whose returns conformed to the Uniform System of Hospital Accounts.

ments either in the form of modest fees, assessed according to income, or through contributory schemes. In 1891 total patients' payments made up only 9 per cent of ordinary income. The proportion had increased to 16 per cent in 1911, 38 per cent in 1921 and 52 per cent in 1938. However, as the PEP report (Table 3) showed, extraordinary payments, particularly in the form of legacies, continued to play an important rôle.

Conclusions

In his book *Capitalism*,[37] Arthur Seldon applied to medical care the analogy of the galloping horse used by Professor E.G. West to describe the intervention of the state in education: the state, he argued, far from providing services not previously available, mounted the already galloping horse of developing private provision in all the main parts of the welfare state.

Examination of primary care services before 1911, as well as primary care for people outside national insurance between 1911 and 1948, and hospital provision up to the Second World War, confirms his thesis. Private medical services had been growing and improving for many decades before the state stepped in. Government had played its part in providing for the very poorest people and, as in all free societies, by keeping in good order the laws which protect human freedom. But the massive and growing scope of private provision shows there was no necessity for the state to monopolise health provision, either in 1911 by compulsory state insurance or in 1948 by state ownership, control or regulation.

---

[37] Oxford: Basil Blackwell, 1990, p.250.

4

HOUSING WITHOUT THE STATE

Martin Ricketts
University of Buckingham

Introduction

NINETEENTH-CENTURY DESCRIPTIONS of insanitary, over-crowded housing conditions so shocked contemporaries that they influenced attitudes to government policy well into the 20th century and colour our responses even on the threshold of the 21st.

Witnesses appearing before the Royal Commission on Housing[1] during 1884 and 1885 appeared to confirm the worst impressions of reformers who could see few signs of improvement. Pamphlets such as George Sims's celebrated 'The Bitter Cry of Outcast London' described the 'pestilential human rookeries' which 'call to mind what we have heard of the middle passage of the slave ship'. Thirty years later in 1917, at the height of the Great War, a Royal Commission on Housing in Scotland[2] reported on the 'occupation of one-room houses by large families, groups of lightless and unventilated houses in the older burghs, clotted masses of slums in the great cities'.

A survey of English housing in 1993-94 produces a contrasting picture – 98 per cent of households with access to one or more rooms per person, 97 per cent of households at or above the 'bedroom standard', 88 per cent very satisfied or fairly satisfied with their accommodation.[3] It seems churlish to talk of a 'lost century' in housing

---

[1] First Report of the Commissioners on the Housing of the Working Classes [England and Wales] 1884-85.

[2] *Report of the Royal Commission on the Housing of the Industrial Population of Scotland Urban and Rural* (1917), Cd.8731, p.346.

[3] Hazel Green and Jacqui Hansbro, *Housing in England 1993/4,* Office of Population Censuses and Surveys, Social Survey Division, London: HMSO, 1994, Tables 2.2, 2.3, 2.4.

policy when, during its course, housing conditions have so dramatically improved. The policy instruments which have accompanied these improvements, however, have produced very substantial distortions to the operation of housing markets. Along with generally rising physical standards brought about by rising incomes there have been misallocations of investment, impediments to labour mobility, disincentives to move house, and distortions to the individual's choice of tenure.

The Range of Government Intervention

So pervasive has been government influence on the housing market that assessing what might have happened in its absence confronts almost insuperable problems. The 20th century has seen continual experiment in housing policy. Rent control[4] was introduced in 1915 and began to be gradually unwound 70 years later in the 1980s. The Local Authority housing sector[5] was established as an important part of housing supply in the years after 1919 but has faced radical reform and numerical decline more recently. The development of town and country planning since 1947 has had an enormous effect on the price and type of housing available. Large slum clearance programmes have transformed whole neighbourhoods and had serious but unanticipated social consequences. The rise of the income tax (paid by only a small fraction of the population at the turn of the 20th century but now by virtually everyone)[6] has had important direct and indirect consequences for the housing market. Periods of severe price deflation between the wars and rapid inflation between the 1960s and the 1980s proved very disruptive to property markets and greatly influenced choice of tenure. A whole range of subsidy instruments, some going to producers (such as renovation grants to landlords and owners), others to consumers (such as housing benefit), have been introduced.

Continual growth in the quality and quantity of dwellings available over the 20th century has therefore been accompanied by large changes in government policy and in the balance between tenure sectors. Figure 1 indicates how the stock of dwellings changed from predominantly rented to predominantly owned between 1914 and 1993. A detailed

---

[4] The Rent and Mortgage Restriction Act 1915.

[5] The Housing and Town Planning Act 1919 was followed by a stream of legislation governing the financial control of Local Authority housebuilding programmes down to the present day.

[6] There were 25·7 million income tax payers in 1994-95.

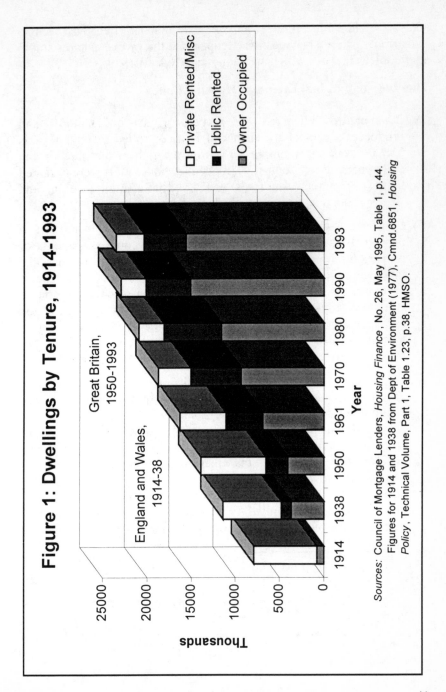

Figure 1: Dwellings by Tenure, 1914-1993

Sources: Council of Mortgage Lenders, *Housing Finance*, No. 26, May 1995, Table 1, p.44. Figures for 1914 and 1938 from Dept of Environment (1977), Cmnd.6851, *Housing Policy*, Technical Volume, Part 1, Table 1.23, p.38, HMSO.

analysis of housing policy would indicate that its effect has been to redistribute income between the occupants of the various tenures and to alter choices in ways which are economically inefficient.

The Redistributional Effects of Housing Policy

(i) Rent control infringed the property rights of landlords and produced a transfer to tenants of rent-controlled dwellings. This transfer was not a simple flow from the rich to the poor. In the early years of rent control 90 per cent of households were in rented homes while many landlords owned and let a single dwelling and were not notably rich relatively to their tenants.[7]

(ii) In Local Authority housing the subsidy system has been in a perpetual state of flux. As the sector grew, complex patterns of redistribution emerged. These were not merely from the national taxpayer to local tenants, they also created transfers from tenants of newer to those of older homes and from local domestic or commercial rate payers to Local Authority tenants.[8] Much of the history of the Local Authority sector in the 20th century can be told in terms of a struggle between different groups of owners and tenants to lay claim to the capital gains on the stock of housing.

(iii) Planning restrictions and 'Green Belts' have raised the price of existing domestic property and forced newcomers into less desirable and more crowded locations. Relatively wealthy groups have asserted their right to environmental amenities the value of which becomes capitalised in the price of their property. Outsiders compete for limited sites on which to live, thus driving up rents and leading to cramped conditions – 'rabbit hutches on postage stamps', as Alan Evans has expressed it.[9] The redistribution of capital and income implied by these forces is regressive from poor to rich, with owners of property in the more desirable locations

---

[7] The Milner Holland Committee reported in 1965 that 60 per cent of landlords in London owned a single property.

[8] L. Rosenthal, 'The Regional and Income Distribution of the Council House Subsidy in the UK', *Manchester School*, Vol.45, 1977, pp.127-40.

[9] Alan Evans, 'Rabbit Hutches on Postage Stamps: Economics, Planning and Development in the 1990s', Discussion Papers in Urban and Regional Economics, Series C, No.55, University of Reading, 1990.

receiving scarcity rents on their artificially limited 'positional goods'.[10]

(iv) The growth in owner-occupation has been associated with spectacular examples of redistribution between owners and tenants. Because owners receive benefits in kind from their housing which have not been subject to tax since 1963, they are able to lay claim to housing on substantially better terms than would be available to tenants because the rent paid to the landlord is taxable. This can be illustrated by imagining a person with £100,000 of financial assets renting a home with a market value of £100,000 from a landlord. Suppose the income from the invested assets just enables the tenant to pay the rent. By exchanging the financial assets for the house the new owner-occupier cuts his tax bill to nothing and continues to live in the house. The erstwhile landlord pays tax on the income from his financial assets in the same way that he before paid tax on the income from the house.[11] The benefit attached to this remission of tax is obviously more valuable the more expensive is the house and the higher the rate of tax on the income generated by assets. It is for these reasons that studies of the impact of income tax provisions on the owner-occupied housing market have always found them to be highly regressive.[12]

The rush into owner-occupation was never more frenetic than in the inflationary era of the 1970s and mid- to late-1980s. During this period real rates of interest were low or even negative. Many savers found it impossible to maintain the value of their capital, while borrowers found the burden of interest payments rapidly diminished with inflationary wage rises. Allowing for capital gains on their housing, borrowers faced a negative cost of capital.[13] Essentially they were receiving a

---

[10] The terminology of 'positional goods' was introduced by F. Hirsch, *The Social Limits to Growth*, London: Routledge and Kegan Paul, 1977.

[11] Complexities concerning responsibility for repairs and maintenance may, of course, affect the outcome.

[12] Recent reductions of mortgage interest tax relief leave the above argument intact. The advantage of owning rather than renting by a borrower is reduced by recent reforms. The advantage of holding net assets in the form of owner-occupied housing rather than other types of assets which generate taxable income remains.

[13] Tim Congdon, 'The housing ladder has fallen down', Gerrard and National, *Monthly Economic Review*, No.29, November 1991.

bounty for living in their own homes. It could not last but, while it did, the redistribution from mortgagee to mortgagor was on an historically large scale.

Twentieth-century housing policy has not merely been redistributive from lower to higher income families. It has affected the allocation of resources in housing and has severely reduced economic efficiency. Following are three examples.

The Effects of Housing Policy on Resource Allocation

(i) Rent controls over a period of 60 years had important consequences for the quality of the stock of housing. When landlords realised that controls were not temporary they responded by reducing maintenance expenditure on their property until the 'quality adjusted' rent once more represented an acceptable return on their investment. Redistribution in favour of the tenant in the short to medium term was offset in the long run by the physical deterioration of rented property. Investment by the state in new dwellings was thus partially vitiated by disinvestment in the private rented sector and the diversion of maintenance expenditure into higher yielding assets elsewhere. New building in the private rented sector virtually ceased after the Second World War.

(ii) Below-market rents in both the local/national government and private sectors reduced labour mobility. By making it more costly to move to new jobs the efficiency of the labour market was reduced and recorded unemployment was higher than it would otherwise have been. A Local Authority tenant, for example, could not move without sacrificing a valuable property right.[14] Only if the right to inhabit a particular dwelling on favourable terms had been tradeable would adverse consequences for mobility have been avoided. The tenant could then have sold the occupation rights to his or her low-rent home for their current value and bought equivalent rights elsewhere. Such trading in occupation rights could have benefited many people in finding employment but was

---

[14] P Minford, P. Ashton, and M. Peel estimated that the national unemployment rate in the mid-1980s was around 2 per cent higher as a result of all rent restrictions than it would have been in their absence: *The Housing Morass: Regulation, Immobility and Unemployment*, Hobart Paperback 25, London: Institute of Economic Affairs, 1987.

illegal and considered scandalous when it was on occasion discovered to have taken place.[15]

(iii) That choice of tenure and home have been greatly influenced by government policy is widely accepted. That the artificial stimulation of particular housing sectors also has had large associated social costs is far less widely appreciated. Attention in popular discussion is so focused on physical housing availability or quality that the precise ways in which property rights are distributed between contracting parties are misleadingly seen as matters of arcane interest to lawyers but of no real economic consequence to ordinary people as owners and tenants. In the real world, such matters go to the heart of the problem of economic organisation in a world of uncertainty. The distribution of risk, the provision of incentives to look after physical assets, the choice of a time-path of saving and dis-saving, the choice of an area, town or country in which to live, and the decision to move – all four aspects of housing are influenced by tenure.

One of the paradoxes of 20th-century housing policy is that the growth of owner-occupation has been seen as a step forward. Yet, as a form of housing tenure, owner-occupation is in some respects rather primitive. Under combined ownership and occupation all the property rights associated with domestic property are held together rather than broken down and apportioned between different people. In particular, it is not obvious why a man or woman who wishes to invest in housing would choose a single property, with all its attendant risks, rather than gaining the advantages of risk pooling by purchasing a small share in a much larger portfolio of housing assets. It is slightly more obvious why he or she might borrow large sums in relation to income in order to invest in housing – the hope of a pure speculative gain. The high 'gearing' associated with the finance of much personal investment in housing adds considerably to the risks which are taken: relatively small proportionate changes in house prices have relatively large proportionate effects on personal 'net worth'. In the past these risks of

---

[15] Establishing trade in occupation rights was suggested for government housing by Samuel Brittan in the mid-1970s and, rather late in the day, for the regulated private sector by Ricketts (1986): Samuel Brittan, *The Economic Consequences of Democracy*, Temple Smith, 1977, pp.170-72; Martin Ricketts, *Lets into Leases: The Political Economy of Rent Deregulation*, London: Centre for Policy Studies, Policy Study No.81, 1986.

TABLE 1:
Mortgage Arrears and Repossessions: UK, 1971-94

	Loans in Arrears		Repossessions
	by 6-12 months	Over 12 months	
1971	17,600		2,800
1976	16,000		5,000
1981	21,500		4,900
1986	52,100	13,000	24,100
1991	183,600	91,700	75,500
1994	153,300	142,200	25,000

Source: *Social Trends*, 1995 Edition, Table 10.17.

home ownership created by government policies have been grossly underestimated. It has taken the upsurge in repossessions and mortgage arrears of recent years (Table 1) to draw attention to them.

Falling house prices in 1990 and 1991 resulted in 'negative equity' for large numbers of recent mortgagors. Many home-owners suffered loss of deposits which may have represented a significant level of savings in relation to their income though less significant relative to the price of the house purchased. Even for those able to service their debt the ability to move will be severely constrained if the proceeds of the sale are not sufficient to pay off the outstanding mortgage. In this way, owner-occupation could cement people into a given location just as firmly as council housing.

Savings decisions are also distorted by favouring owner-occupation above other forms of tenure. During the inflationary years of the 1970s the advantages of getting to the bottom rung of the 'housing ladder' distorted the natural life-time patterns of saving. Rapid accumulation of capital in the form of housing at a young age is not attempted in other countries such as Germany or Switzerland where the state has remained more neutral between the different forms of tenure. There, people expect to buy housing in their forties rather than in their twenties. Dis-saving in retirement is also discouraged when assets are held in the form of housing rather than more easily realisable financial instruments.

Public Choice and Housing Tenure

In a democratic polity the expression 'housing without the state' sounds like a paradox. Housing capital cannot at low cost be used for other purposes. In the short to medium term, therefore, much of the return to housing is a 'quasi rent' – a payment in excess of the minimum required to keep the assets deployed in the housing market.

This huge pool of rent is vulnerable to various forms of rent-seeking through the political process.

- *First*, taxpayers vie with tenants for rents on the government stock of housing.

- *Second*, tenants of old local council property seek to claim the capital gains on the stock by keeping rents low or purchasing at privileged prices.

- *Third*, tenants of private sector landlords try to lay claim to some of the rental flow on that stock by means of rent regulation.

- *Fourth*, owners try to create scarcity rents by lobbying for restrictions on new housing development.

- *Fifth*, owners oppose the taxation of the implicit rents received from their property.

It is difficult to see why any of this political pressure on local or national government should change in the near future, unless all voters begin to perceive the net costs of their combined activity and select candidates offering less intervention all round. It is as likely, however, that public choice forces will lead to continuing instability in the housing market as different interests combine to oppose one another.[16]

Yet if disengagement of government from the housing market were possible, the results would be far reaching. The history of housing in the 20th century would have been substantially different if direct housing provision at below-market rents and regulatory and fiscal intervention had been avoided.

What Kind of Housing System Might Have Evolved?

A market relatively free of the large-scale interference described earlier might have been expected to produce a distinctly different set of

---

[16] This possibility is discussed more fully in M. Ricketts, 'Housing Policy and Public Choice', *Wincott Discussion Paper 08/95*, School of Business, University of Buckingham, 1995.

outcomes. A drift towards owner-occupation might have occurred anyway as incomes rose and inflationary pressure made people look for a good store of value. But, in general, the choice of tenure would have been far more dependent on three considerations: risk sharing; reducing costs of transacting; and providing efficient incentives to maintenance.

In this context it is unlikely that mobile or relatively poor people would find owner-occupation a suitable form of tenure. Even the fairly affluent might have continued the tradition of living in rented property. It is a matter for conjecture, however, whether large-scale property companies might have increased in importance relative to the small local landlord. Such companies would have permitted more professional management to develop and would have had risk-pooling advantages for providers of rented housing. The problem of monitoring the tenant's treatment of the property and agreeing on responsibility for maintenance would, however, have militated against such companies and in favour of owner-occupation and the growth of the building societies.

In the sphere of 'social' housing – the provision of homes for the poorest and least advantaged in the population – the consequences of a less active state would have been substantial. In the first place, the effect of subsidies to the middle classes combined with strict planning restrictions on new development has been to raise the price of land. Whatever benefits the zoning and planning restrictions of the post-war world may have produced, they have made the provision of affordable housing for the relatively poor far more difficult than it might otherwise have been.

So closely associated was the provision of 'social' housing during the 1950s and 1960s with large-scale slum clearance conducted by local authorities that alternative mechanisms for improvement were bypassed. A deregulated market might have been expected to result in more evolutionary change, smaller scale redevelopment and far more use of renovation rather than clearance. The understandable political impatience to be rid of unfit dwellings would not have found an outlet. But some of the socially destructive experiment with high density, high-rise housing would have been avoided.

With rising incomes, housing conditions for most people would have improved without state assistance. Greater variety in contractual arrangements in housing might have been expected as people sought to satisfy their differing requirements: security of tenure, mobility, standards of service, investment potential, financial safety, and so forth. For the poorest groups the activities of local or national charitable associations or Housing Associations would have been important. Ultimately there is no escaping the view that if there is a demand for 'slum' housing a market will produce it. It would, however, be a mistake to conclude that, but for large-scale state action, the 'pestilential human rookeries' of the mid-19th century would have been perpetuated on a large scale through to the end of the 20th. In a less regulated and distorted market, smaller scale assistance from local and national government might have achieved more for the poor.

5

UNEMPLOYMENT INSURANCE WITHOUT THE STATE

Michael Beenstock

Hebrew University of Jerusalem, Israel

A CENTURY AGO PRIVATE INSURANCE MARKETS in health, unemployment and other benefits were developing in the wake of revolutions in medical science and industry. It is my contention that, left to themselves, these markets would have continued to develop so that by today there would have been a thriving market providing sophisticated insurance contracts for unemployment contingencies just as the market has provided insurance for a vast range of other contingencies. There would have been nothing special about unemployment insurance but for the fact that ever since the National Insurance Act of 1911 it became a target for nationalisation when unemployment insurance, together with other forms of insurance, was 'socialised'. The development of private unemployment insurance markets was nipped in the bud.

To create a better future we need to further our understanding of the past. Why did the Social Insurance revolution come about during the first decade of the 20th century? Why were private insurance markets not left to grow and flower? Why 1911 rather than a quarter of a century sooner or later?

To answer these questions we must first look to the welfare state precedent set by Bismarck in the 1880s. Bismarck justified his State Socialism in terms of both religion and *realpolitik*. It was *realpolitik* that really motivated him; he had banned socialist parties in 1878 and his State Socialism was intended to placate the working classes and to avoid a socialist revolution.[1] The state provided accident, health and

---

[1] Otto Pflanze, *Bismarck and the Development of Modern Germany*, Vol. III, Ch. 6, New Haven, CT: Princeton University Press, 1990.

pension insurance but it signally avoided unemployment insurance. Germany subsequently become the conscious model for Lloyd George, Beveridge and Churchill. Beveridge visited Germany to study its welfare arrangements in 1907 and Lloyd George in 1908.

Why this sudden interest in Germany? In Gilbert's opinion, what motivated Bismarck also motivated reformers in Britain, especially after the extension of the franchise to working-class men in 1885.

> 'Great Britain was diverted from a socialist solution to the problem of poverty and was turned instead to the establishment of the institution of social insurance. The profit system, with its vagaries and caprices, was left intact.'[2]

Beveridge's motives were most probably somewhat different, although he too was concerned with finding the Third Way. According to José Harris, before the First World War Beveridge saw no conflict between state action and free enterprise:

> 'Indeed, like Edwin Chadwick he seems to have believed that, far from damaging the free market, interventionist social policies could structure and strengthen the free market, and render it more efficient than ever before.'[3]

Furthermore, there is no indication in his *Unemployment: a Problem of Industry*, published in 1909, that he was aware of such a conflict. He was naïve.

London's Poor

Since Beveridge was the architect of the path-breaking National Insurance Act of 1911, it is worth reflecting on how he reached his conclusions. Having been exposed to London's poor during his years at Toynbee Hall, he embarked on an inductive empirical analysis of poverty. In doing so he was impressed by the fact that unemployment insurance was provided by trade unions.[4] But instead of leaving this market to develop he decided that it should be taken over by the state. At the time he gave no reason why state intervention was necessary. Indeed, the Webbs were against it, preferring instead that private

---

[2] B.B. Gilbert, *The Evolution of National Insurance in Great Britain*, London: Michael Joseph, 1966, p.451.

[3] J. Harris, *William Beveridge*, Oxford: Clarendon Press, 1977, p.472.

[4] Indeed, in *Unemployment: a Problem of Industry* (pp.223-30), he provides a very positive account of what he learnt.

insurance should be encouraged by subsidies (the so-called Ghent system) which were justified since they helped to reduce the Poor Rate. Much later in his *Social Insurance and Allied Services* (1942) he attacked (pp.29-30) private insurance in favour of Social Insurance, but this is a different matter.

Why did not Beveridge leave well alone in 1907-10? Correlli Barnett[5] sees Beveridge as another Utopian and 'New Jerusalemer', a product of his Victorian education destined to improve the world. Indeed, José Harris writes[6] that

> 'Beveridge's ideal society, he confided to an LSE audience in 1934, would be run not by dictators nor by parliamentary democracy but by professional administrators or "social doctors".'

This view of Beveridge was confirmed by Harold Wilson who remarked in the 1966 Beveridge Memorial Lecture that Beveridge considered 'all problems are soluble given enough staff'. In November 1939 Beveridge himself remarked: 'The choice is no longer between Utopia and the pleasant ordered world that our fathers knew. The choice is between Utopia and Hell.'[7] Although these words were uttered in the context of the abolition of war, they might equally have applied to his ambition to abolish poverty.

Beveridge and the 1911 Act

In short, it was the fateful combination of Beveridge and the political climate in Edwardian Britain that spelt doom for private unemployment insurance as well as other aspects of private insurance. Beveridge on his own could not have done it. Nor could Lloyd George and Churchill without Beveridge at the Board of Trade. Also the timing of the Royal Commission on the Poor Laws which reported in 1909 was fortuitous. The hearings provided Beveridge with a stage to present his ideas, and he carried the Commission with him. Had the Commission reported in, say, 1906 matters might have been different. The 1911 Act was an historical accident that was to set the tone for the rest of the 20th century.

By the early 1940s Beveridge had revised his view:

---

[5] *The Audit of War*, London: Macmillan, 1986.

[6] *Op. cit.*, p.472.

[7] Quoted on p.353 of his autobiography, *Power and Influence*, London: Hodder and Stoughton, 1953.

'The State in organizing society should not stifle incentive, opportunity, responsibility; in establishing a national minimum, it should leave room and encouragement for voluntary action by each individual to provide more than the minimum for himself and his family.'[8]

But it was too late. In the case of unemployment insurance, private incentive had been stifled. Six years later, in his *Voluntary Action* (1948), Beveridge called for a revival of voluntarism and the friendly societies alongside Social Insurance but he failed to understand that the two were incompatible. His Third Report is riddled with contradictions and betrays an abject failure to understand the behaviour of private markets under conditions of extensive state intervention. Moreover, he was anti-business, and in specific reference to the assurance industry he had this to say:

'The business motive is a good servant but a bad master, and a society which gives itself up to the dominance of the business motive is a bad society.'[9]

Riding the Kuznets Roller Coaster

According to the late Nobel laureate, Simon Kuznets, the process of industrialisation tends to reduce the share of the poor in national income during its early stages. As the process of industrialisation matures the distribution of income tends to become more equal and the share of the lower income deciles tends to improve. This may be understood in terms of the development model proposed by another Nobel laureate, W. Arthur Lewis, who argued that in the early stages of economic development there is an almost infinitely elastic supply of cheap labour from the countryside prepared to migrate to industrial jobs in the towns. During this stage owners of capital are the main beneficiaries of industrialisation. Once the rural reservoir of cheap labour starts to dry up, however, the terms of trade move in favour of labour; labour becomes a sellers' market and the distribution of income tends to move in its favour.

The political problem of economic development is somehow to get across the bottom of the 'Kuznets Curve' without a revolution or other

---

[8] W.H. Beveridge, *Social Insurance and Allied Services*, Cmd. 6404, London: HMSO, 1942, p.67.

[9] *Voluntary Action*, London: Allen and Unwin, 1948, p.322.

action that jeopardises the entry into mature capitalism. The 1911 revolution should be seen as an attempt to ride the rapids of the 'Kuznets Curve' in Britain. Elsewhere, as in Russia in 1917, failure to ride the 'Kuznets Curve' had more serious consequences.

In a mature capitalist economy there is no need for the desperate measures taken at the bottom of the 'Kuznets Curve'. The time has long since arrived to let private insurance markets take over from social insurance where they left off at the beginning of the century. In unemployment insurance the government should gradually reduce its rôle to pave the way for a healthy market in private unemployment insurance contracts. This has been happening extensively in pensions and to a lesser extent in health. It is time to turn attention to unemployment insurance. Britain was the first to socialise unemployment insurance in 1911. There would be poetic justice if she was the first to desocialise it.

Actuarial Foundations

In 1986 Valerie Brasse and I set out the actuarial foundations for the competitive pricing of unemployment insurance contracts.[10] The basic idea is simple: the unemployed should receive the benefits for which they have paid and the premium should reflect the risks that are underwritten. In short, unemployment insurance would be no different from motor car insurance or any other type of insurance. The Nobel laureate, Friedrich Hayek, had a similar view:

> 'There is undoubtedly a case for genuine insurance against unemployment wherever practical, insurance in which the different risks of the various trades are reflected in the premiums paid.'[11]

People working in jobs where unemployment risks are higher would pay higher premiums, as they did before 1911. Customers would be free to choose between policies offering different degrees of cover. Policies entitling the insured to draw benefit for a longer period would be more expensive. In the book we presented illustrative calculations of what such policies might look like. This is, of course, no substitute for

---

[10] M. Beenstock and V. Brasse, *Insurance for Unemployment*, London: Allen & Unwin in association with the IEA, 1986; also my article with D. Blake, 'Stochastic Analysis of Competitive Unemployment Insurance Pricing', *European Economic Review*, Vol.32, 1988, p.726.

[11] F.A. Hayek, *The Constitution of Liberty*, London: Routledge & Kegan Paul, 1960, p.301.

the real thing that would be provided in a competitive private market. Nevertheless, I believe that our proposal sets out a market alternative to Beveridge's social insurance and should provide the basis for policy in the 21st century.

Pricing Formula

Our actuarial pricing formula comprised the following components:

- *Risk Classification* – Workers were distinguished by both their propensity to enter unemployment and their subsequent propensity to leave unemployment. These propensies were found to vary by age, sex, occupation, region, family status and industry.

- *Terms of Benefit* – Unemployment insurance contracts may have different terms relating to the risk period during which the job loss is insured, the benefit period during which the claimant may draw unemployment pay, and the level of benefit.

- *Interest Rates* – Since premiums are paid before benefits are drawn insurance companies gain from higher interest rates. Hence premiums should vary inversely with the rate of interest.

- *Diversification and Reinsurance* – Because of macro-economic factors unemployment risks in different industries tend to rise and fall together, which makes risk-spreading more difficult. However, since the economic cycle in, say, the UK is not perfectly correlated with the cycle in other countries, further diversification is available through the international market in reinsurance. UK macro-economic risk can be almost entirely diversified away in a portfolio of world risk which includes unemployment alongside a host of other risks. The book uses practical examples to show that premiums vary directly with the degree of risk and benefits and inversely with interest rates and diversifiability.

Depoliticisation Gains

Returning unemployment insurance to the market is not suggested simply for its own sake. The main benefit will take the form of gains in efficiency primarily through depoliticisation. In a private market, unemployment benefit could not be open-ended. It is my contention that, but for the 1911 misjudgement by politicians and their advisers, rational unemployment policies would have been marketed which would have avoided the mistakes of social insurance – high replacement ratios and excessive benefit periods – that only politicians could afford to make. Private competition would have driven premiums and benefits into sensible proportion as in other kinds of insurance. The over-generous provision of unemployment benefit by the state has harmed work incentives and created an unemployment problem. The face of unemployment would have been entirely different had private unemployment insurance markets been left to develop naturally in and after 1911.

To cite some home-grown evidence in favour of the importance of limiting the amount of time for which benefit may be drawn, I refer to the experience in Israel where unemployment benefit is available for only six months. Once the six months are up the unemployed have to take whatever job is going even if the pay is low. Because of immigration from the CIS (formerly the USSR), the labour force has swollen by some 20 per cent since 1989, yet the rate of unemployment is lower now than it was in 1989 after having risen in the meanwhile by about 2 percentage points. *The finite benefit period is the cause of the miracle.* No doubt if Britain were to be inundated by, say, 6 million immigrants within a few years, the unemployment rate would rise by about 10 percentage points because the unemployment benefit system is open-ended.

After more than 80 years we have naturally grown accustomed to thinking that unemployment insurance is the province of the state rather than the market. But this is no more than an habitual mode of thought which we take for granted until we awake from our stupor. Some, Beveridge included, have argued that unemployment risks are different from any other type of insurable risk and that the market is bound to fail in the provision of satisfactory contracts. This is because unemployment is a macro-economic phenomenon; the risks that the individual faces are systemic – a worker can lose his job because some third party has gone bankrupt, because of a recession in another industry or even country, or because of a change in monetary and fiscal policy. Moreover, there is a high correlation between unemployment risks; unemployment has its own epidemiology – it comes in waves and is contagious. In short, unemployment risks are special.

Unemployment Risks No More Special Than Motor

We could just as easily persuade ourselves that motor insurance was special. The determinants of road accidents are systemic too, depending on general public behaviour in road use, driving speed, networks and such-like. Moreover, policy on speed limits and road investment determines the risk exposure of the individual. The analogy is complete; there is no more case for socialising unemployment insurance than there is for socialising motor insurance. There may be a case for making some unemployment insurance compulsory, just as third-party motor insurance is compulsory. But this is a different issue. It is true that unemployment risks in different occupations are positively correlated, but they are far from being perfectly or even highly correlated. As already noted, positive correlation might make unemployment insurance more expensive but this in itself is nothing special.

The social insurance lobby has also claimed that although social and private insurance co-exist in health, disability and pensions, and private education co-exists with state education, the private sector has failed to provide supplementary unemployment insurance. This, they argue, testifies to the market's inability to cover unemployment risks. This argument is wrong for several reasons.

- *First*, if the standard of provision by the state were high there would be no demand for supplementary private provision. If the state schools were excellent there would still be some, but not much, demand for private education. For the majority this has happened in unemployment insurance; because the benefits are generous there is for most people no supplementary demand for private provision.

- *Second*, before its socialisation in 1911, private unemployment insurance existed and was developing.

- *Third*, it is not true that private supplementary provision does not exist. For most of us it comes disguised as insured mortgages. We insure the payments on our mortgages because we desire the security of housing tenure. The main risk that we are insuring against is our inability to cover our mortgage payments in the event of unemployment. The mortgage insurance industry is massive; without it the duress of unemployed owner-occupiers would have been considerably greater.

The 21st Century

The short-termism and myopia of Beveridge, Lloyd George and Churchill have cost us a century in social progress. They failed to ride the Kuznets Roller Coaster. To be fair, they most probably could not have appreciated the character and dynamics of modern economic growth even if they had had the inclination. It is easy to be wise after Kuznets, Lewis and others. At the time, Marx must have seemed pretty convincing, and Beveridge and others desperately tried to find the Third Way.

The shock-waves of history die away slowly. This is true for the former communist countries that tried the Second Way and it is true for countries like Britain which tried the Third Way. The bottom of the Kuznets Curve has long since passed. The pressures that gave birth to the Third Way are now history. As we face the 21st century the time has come to rethink social policy. We need a new Beveridge and Lloyd George to undo the process they began in 1911 so that by 2011 the First Way will provide the basis for unemployment insurance – and allied services – to replace the welfare state.

The Tactics of Reform: 'Gradualism' and 'Maximalism'

The 20th century was a lost century; much ground has to be recovered. This will be all the more difficult for two interrelated reasons: because unemployment insurance in Britain was among the first casualties of the welfare state, and because the rate of unemployment is very high. Society has indulged itself for so long that change is bound to be especially difficult.

The economic study of transition has tended to polarise into two conflicting branches. 'Maximalism' is based on the idea of cold shock therapy; 'gradualism' assumes the patient will do better in the long run if he is allowed more time to adjust. The maximalists claim that interest groups are given too much time to thwart the transition process if change is too gradual. Indeed, the rise of the welfare state after the Second World War was based on maximalism rather than gradualism. It was in some sense easier to nationalise the health service, the means of production, and social insurance as a package than it was to nationalise one of them on its own.

In privatising unemployment insurance it makes a big difference if it forms an integral part of the general dismantlement of the welfare state, or whether it is an initiative which stands on its own. If the former, the process becomes relatively simple because many different vested interests are both losers and gainers at the same time. So group *A* may gain from the action taken against *B* but lose from the action taken against itself, while group *B* may gain from the action taken against *A* but lose from the action taken against itself. If maximalist action is taken which adversely affects both *A* and *B*, they may elect to acquiesce because they both stand to gain from the action taken against the other. If, however, a minimalist agenda is adopted, and action is taken only against *A*, it will engage in collective action to defend itself with possibly sufficient effect to thwart the reform.

The unemployed and people employed but facing high unemployment risk naturally stand most to lose from the return of unemployment insurance to the market-place. I believe their resistance will be less within a maximalist context of reform. I therefore devote my closing remarks to feasible action that might be taken if the reform of unemployment insurance stands on its own within a 'minimalist' strategy. It goes without saying that the complete privatisation of unemployment insurance should be undertaken within a maximalist context.

I start from the minimum 'minimorum' and work upwards from there:

1. In countries, such as Britain, where entitlement to unemployment benefit is effectively open-ended, an upper limit on the duration of entitlement should be imposed, ideally about six months, a reasonable period of time to search the labour market. This step is important because private unemployment insurance contracts will not be open-ended. It is no accident that countries such as the USA and Israel, with reasonable upper limits on the duration of entitlement, experience, on average, lower rates of unemployment than countries, such as the UK, where the opposite applies.

2. State-provided unemployment benefit should be minimal in the same way that countries have tended to provide minimal pensions. Individuals may top-up their unemployment insurance cover in the private sector just as workers top-up their pension in the private sector. In the UK, for example, the phasing out of the State Earnings Related Pensions Scheme (SERPS) serves as a prototype for the phasing out of State Earnings Related Unemployment Benefit (SERUB). The minimal unemployment benefit will not be earnings-related in order to encourage higher earners to buy topping-up from private unemployment insurance agents. The analogy between SERPS and SERUB is complete.

3. National insurance contributions should be itemised with a separate heading for unemployment insurance. Contributors should be made

aware of their outlay on the premia they pay for unemployment insurance.

4. The Government Actuary should classify insurance risks, and workers in higher risk groups should pay higher contributions. These premia should be actuarially fair estimates of the true premia, and may be calculated along the lines suggested by Valerie Brasse and me in our book. If the Government Actuary happens to overcharge it will encourage private suppliers of unemployment insurance.

These steps form part of a second-best programme of reform based on gradualism. The key objective is to reduce the rôle of government to a minimum, leaving the private sector to fill the gap opened up by the retreat of the state.

The damage of a century of social insurance will be difficult, but not impossible, to rectify.

6

PENSIONS WITHOUT THE STATE

Arthur Seldon

IN 1957 THE INSTITUTE'S FIRST PAPER on provision for life-time contingencies – loss of income in ill-health, interruptions in employment and retirement – questioned the *rationale* of the expansion since 1925 in state pensions financed by compulsory 'National' Insurance contributions. Since then state pensions, financed less by contributions but instead increasingly by taxes, have become one of the four main components of the political creation romanticised into the 'welfare' state. The others are education, medical care and housing.

Richly varied methods of saving have long been used voluntarily by the British people to prepare for the uncertainties of life. Although many in the 1870s (and earlier) earned low incomes, they had sacrificed current consumption to prepare for future risks to help themselves and their families.

In 1957, only nine years after the establishment of the post-war welfare state, it was timely to assert that '...rights to pensions are not the only supports to which people can look forward in their old age'. Private saving in many forms had created large reserves of

> 'private property, which offers a more certain basis for security in old age than the State and its pensions. They comprise a large accumulation of wealth out of which provision for retirement can be made. And more and more people are accumulating wealth in these forms'.[1]

The Early Growth of Private Saving

This voluntary saving originated in the decisions of individuals of all income-groups, including many with low earnings, in the 70 years and more since the middle-late 19th century. It revealed widespread

---

[1] A. Seldon, *Pensions in a Free Society*, London: Institute of Economic Affairs, 1957, pp.5, 67 (Table II, including the notes).

providence, often in association with other people in the same occupations or other like circumstances, assertion of the dignity and pride of independence, concern for family.

The estimates of private saving in the 1950s were derived from compilations from the most reliable information available, by academic researchers, savings organisations and government departments. They found that millions of people were saving, some or possibly many in several ways, and had accumulated private property, in both financial instruments like savings accounts, insurance policies and stocks and shares ('liquid assets') and in real estate like homes and other property ('non-liquid assets') of roughly £34-35,000 million. (The Gross National Product in 1950-1955 was around £15,000 million.) There were multiple holdings in more than one kind of saving and sometimes several accounts opened by individual owners. The number of owners was known fairly precisely in some categories, like the 4·6 million owners of the homes they occupied, but less in others, like the owners of multiple savings accounts.

In all, the estimates indicated 23 million Post Office Savings Bank Accounts, eight million Trustee Savings Bank Accounts, millions of Defence Bonds, National Savings Certificates and Premium Savings Bonds to a total value of around £4,500 million. There were evidently around 3.5 million holdings of Building Society Shares and Deposits, some 14 million accounts with Industrial and Provident Societies, including Co-operative Societies, and over eight million accounts with Friendly Societies.

£2,000 million to £2,500 million were held in bank deposits, between £10,500 and £11,000 million in stocks and shares, and £3,000 million to £3,500 million in Government securities apart from Defence Bonds and National Savings Certificates (above).

Over 4.5 million homes (housing perhaps 10 million people) worth £6,500 million were owned by the occupiers. Land valued at £1,000 million was owned privately.

Not least, there were large holdings of assurance policies and annuities. Over 88 million industrial assurance policies and annuities worth nearly £900 million were held with assurance companies and 33 million worth nearly £250 million with Collecting Societies. A further nine million policies and annuities worth £2,275 million were held with life assurance companies. And savings of some £2,000 million were held in the form of household goods, business assets and other property.

Some of these figures were more or less precise, others were the then most available estimates. They seem to have been the best approximations to private saving a few years after the post-war expansion in the welfare state. Of the total population of 50 million, many with lower incomes, several million were evidently saving and accumulating property to meet the risks of loss of earnings.

There had also been expansion, mainly since the 1930s, in the number of men and women covered in pension schemes for retirement organised by their employers (though their cost could partly be passed on to other producers and consumers) as part of their working arrangements called 'occupational' pensions. In 1951 they covered two and a third million employed by government and nearly four million by private industry, a total of 6¼ million, nearly five million men and 1.3 million women.[2]

These pensions in private industry had generally begun in the 1930s, mostly among people paid by salary, but during the 1950s and 1960s they spread fairly far down the income scale to employees paid by wages. In recent years occupational pensions have covered in all around a half of the work-force of some 25 million. Saving by pensions came later than by the other methods listed above, but it embraced people with lower as well as higher incomes.

The Politics of Pensions

It must have been clear to students of the subject in the early 1950s, as well as to politicians and their civil service advisers responsible for extending the state pensions that would affect families for 20, 30, 40 or more years ahead, that most people in all income groups were accumulating savings and property available to provide income in their retirement, directly by pensions or annuities and indirectly by savings and private property.

Only a few years earlier, in 1948, the post-war Labour Government must have known of these voluntary private alternatives to compulsory state pensions, especially the Prime Minister, (Major) Clement Attlee, the middle-class social worker at Toynbee Hall in the East End of London, and his Ministers of working-class origin like Ernest Bevin and Aneurin Bevan who had benefited from them in their family lives. Yet they ignored the genesis of this saving: the fundamental trait in the British character of independence and self-respect and the instinct to

---

[2] *Ibid.*, p.4 (Table I).

combine in communities with common interests such as Friendly Societies to safeguard their families. Instead, the Government enlarged the original 1908 'Old-Age' tax-financed pension and the 1925 National Insurance pension into the 1948 Retirement Pension that was to be financed by National Insurance contributions but has ended in being paid for increasingly out of taxation.

The 1948 extension of the state pension originated what became perhaps the most damaging conflict in post-war British society between the political process and the growing saving habits of the people. All employers and employees were required to pay 'National Insurance' contributions. This technical term concealed what was revealed in the end as a fundamentally fraudulent description for the tax that government in later years was induced to raise successively to help avoid openly described taxation, direct on incomes and indirect on purchases, and the borrowing required to pay for rising government expenditures, not least on other state welfare services, especially medical care and education.

The Classical Warning

Almost exactly a hundred years ago, in 1893, Alfred Marshall, the Cambridge economist who taught classical truths before his University succumbed to the political expedient of Keynesian full employment at all costs, told the Royal Commission on the Aged Poor to resist the 'universal pensions' advised by the Fabians, Sidney and Beatrice Webb. He warned they 'do not contain...the seeds of their own disappearance. I am afraid that, if started, they would tend to become perpetual'.

He has been proved right. Even as upright an economist-turned-politician as Hugh Gaitskell could not resist misusing Beveridge's dangerous toy, the higher National Insurance pension, for political purposes by starting it almost from the first year rather than waiting until the National Insurance Fund had been built up over 20 years, as Beveridge had earlier advised (and as a private pension fund would have had to accumulate). The excuse, that the pensioners could not wait years for higher incomes, was unconvincing since people in most need could have been assisted from general taxes without encumbering the National Insurance Fund with uninsured liabilities and expenditures.

It was an unfortunate precedent, and it contributed substantially to the financial deterioration in National Insurance. Later Ministers of Pensions or Social Security faced acute embarrassment. Another academic-turned-politician, Richard Crossman, exchanged the accusation of 'swindling'[3] with John Boyd Carpenter, his political opposite number, when in the 1960s both turned to graduating contributions in the vain effort to save the National Insurance Fund from becoming what it had been for some years – not a fund but a tank, emptied almost as soon as it was refilled.

Financial deregulation has enabled employers and employees to change from occupational to personal pensions, with advantages to both but also predictable abuses that accompany innovations where 'amateur' buyers are initially less informed than 'professional' sellers. To judge these abuses, the market 'imperfections', which are coming to light after a few short years, have to be set beside the government 'imperfections' – the wastes, inflexibility, inflation and deception in state pensions which have taken decades to be discovered and will take more decades to remove.

State Pensions Are Out of Date

The longer the basic state pension takes to be run down as more flexible private pensions and other forms of saving are preferred, the earlier the process should begin. The beginning has been urged since 1957.[4] The Government recently announced the beginning to start 60 years later in AD 2017. Such is the inflexibility of the state, which arouses expectations and produces governments tempted to take the short view about the dates of general elections, and puts the long view a poor second.

Whether private saving would have continued to expand if the state had not introduced its pensions in 1908, 1925, and 1948 is properly debatable. Nor can it be said with certainty that the increase would have been enough to dispense with the pensions introduced by the state. It is arguable that the less provident would not have saved in the expectation that a compassionate society would support them in impecunious old age, or that their more affluent children would pay for their homes and living costs. We shall never know because the necessity to save was lessened by the state pension system.

---

[3] A. Seldon, *The Great Pensions Swindle*, London: Tom Stacey, 1970.

[4] A. Seldon, *The State is Rolling Back*, London: E. & L. Books in association with the IEA, 1994.

Yet it is implausible to suppose that the saving institutions formed from the 1870s and earlier, based on the habits of thrift, providence, family solidarity, and self-respect, would have weakened or died out.

Towards the Future

The history of what happened does not throw conclusive light on what would have happened to private provision for retirement if conditions had become more favourable to voluntary saving by the earlier winding-up of compulsory saving through the state. Yet rising real incomes, the unprecedented advance in living standards, the accelerated leisure pursuits, lengthening life-expectancy and the advancing years of working life beyond the artificial retirement ages of state schemes – all these perhaps unexpected trends point to the most supportable conclusion: that private saving and assurance through the long-established mutual and profit-oriented institutions, investment through unit and investment trusts, deposits in building societies and banks, private property in homes and newer ways of saving would have continued to expand in the last 60 years.

Not least, the more the market was allowed to devise new methods of preparing for comfortable retirement, the more competition in a free market would have invigorated the traditional institutions to modernise their methods and marketing. And the more the difficulty of governments in maintaining their pensions for growing numbers of state pensioners, the more the nation will have lost in repressing the varied vehicles of private saving, and the more we should now welcome their rebirth and recovery.

The governments of the main European countries are gradually and painfully accepting that they will be unable to provide the state pensions they have long promised their people.

In Britain, it is only since the 1970s that both major parties have attempted to extract more money in graduated insurance contributions in exchange for equal pensions. Both were at pains to find new justifications for this misuse of the national 'insurance' system to justify redistributive taxation. Yet doubts were surfacing earlier in the 1960s. Ministers of both political parties showed anxiety. After several *Hobart* and other IEA papers in its early years on pensions, Margaret Herbison, Labour Secretary of State, and John Boyd-Carpenter, the Conservative Minister, asked the author for talks. Both seemed uneasy, but the time for courageous reform was apparently not yet. It would have required the 'appalling candour' that Baldwin had to confess in the 1930s when he had failed to reveal that his party had not taken the public into its confidence on rearmament in the face of the Hitler threat of war in Europe.

But in 1996 the time for appalling candour has arrived. The people are having to be told that they would be wise to begin saving privately in their middle working years for their retirement 15 or 20 years later at age 65. And the system of national insurance for pensions income in retirement is belatedly drawing to its close. But its lesson must be learned: pensions cannot be left to the political process with its short time-horizons and its temptation to tax or borrow to disguise its inability to create the welfare services the people would prefer.

Not least, if they had been left to develop their private saving they could now look forward to more secure years of retirement.

SELF-HELP: THE INSTINCT TO ADVANCE

Charles Hanson
University of Newcastle upon Tyne

'The spirit of self-help is the root of all genuine growth in the individual; and exhibited in the lives of many, it constitutes the true source of national vigour and strength.'

Samuel Smiles, *Self-Help*, London: John Murray, 1859.[1]

'Emphasis on duty rather than assertion of rights presents itself today as the condition on which alone humanity can resume the progress in civilization ... interrupted by two world wars.'

Lord Beveridge, *Voluntary Action*, London: Allen and Unwin, 1948.

THOSE WHO AUTOMATICALLY PUT ON THE LIGHT as they step into a dark room should occasionally ponder the question of how people managed before the invention of electricity. After all, it became widely available only 60 years ago. In the same way it is good to think about the ways in which people on very low incomes (the large majority) managed before the introduction of the 'welfare' state, which arrived only a few years before electricity. How on earth did they cope with such large families, especially during the inevitable periods of sickness, unemployment and old age?

Sometimes they could not cope. The infant mortality rate was much higher than today; diphtheria (among others) was a deadly disease; and it was common for women to die in childbirth. But many large families managed on incomes which were tiny in comparison with those of

---

[1] Samuel Smiles, *Self-Help*, London: Institute of Economic Affairs, 1996 (First Edn., 1859).

today. And, most surprising of all, after practically all working men were given the vote by the Reform Acts of 1867 and 1884, only a minority wanted the state to step in and provide benefits to cosset them from womb to tomb. Perhaps they had a more sensible and realistic view of politicians than we have today. Perhaps they had the sneaking suspicion that most political promises were empty and that they would end up paying for many, if not all, of the benefits themselves through the tax system.

However, if they were doubtful about state intervention, they were extremely enthusiastic about self-help. Samuel Smiles's book, *Self-Help*, not only sold by the thousand; it provided the inspiration for a wide range of voluntary services, whose extent has usually been much under-estimated, even by social historians. The best known of these were the friendly societies,[2] which normally provided sickness and death benefits for a contribution of about sixpence a week. These were the two benefits most people wanted, and sixpence a week was what they could afford and were willing to pay.

Minimal Waste

The friendly societies were controlled by the members and managed in their interests, so waste was minimal; and, with benefits monitored by friends and workmates of the recipients, scrounging was almost impossible. The government had provided for the voluntary registration of friendly societies and most of the largest, such as the Manchester Unity of Odd Fellows and the Hearts of Oak, had registered. But because registration was voluntary there were many unregistered, and this meant that even an eminent scholar like Lord Beveridge underestimated the total number of friendly society members in 1910, just as the 'welfare state' was being inaugurated, when he wrote that there were about four and three-quarter million members in that year. This figure ignored the numerous members in unregistered societies and was a substantial under-estimate.[3] The true total was probably at least 8 million and could have been even higher.

The truth was that the friendly society movement was even more vigorous than its friends realised. By 1910 a very large majority of adult males were members, and therefore covered by sick and death

---

[2] See Chapter 8 of this *Readings*.

[3] C.G. Hanson, 'Welfare before the Welfare State', Ch. 5 of *The Long Debate on Poverty*, IEA Readings No. 9, London: Institute of Economic Affairs, 1972, pp.112-34.

benefits. Also, as friendly society membership was growing faster than the population, non-members were a constantly diminishing minority. As E.W. Brabrook, the Registrar of Friendly Societies, had put it in evidence to the Aberdare Commission on the Aged Poor in 1893:

> 'It would look as if there was really merely a kind of residuum left of those who are in uncertain work or otherwise, and are not able to insure in some degree or another.'

That 'residuum' was the real problem which had to be dealt with at the turn of the 20th century. The tragedy of the 'welfare state' is that the reformers have been far more interested in grandiose, centralised, all-embracing compulsory schemes than in tackling the tricky problem of the 'residuum'. And in developing these grandiose schemes they have damaged the spirit of self-help, of which the friendly societies were the epitome.

It is impossible to estimate precisely the size of 'the residuum' who had not joined a friendly society by 1910, but it was probably not more than 10 per cent of the adult male population. We need to ask why this small minority was acting as it did, and the answers are fairly obvious. Some of them suffered chronic ill-health; others were casual labourers with no regular income (and perhaps preferred this kind of life-style); yet others made regular (daily) contributions to the profits of the brewers instead of providing for the possibility of ill-health or unemployment. The Victorians divided this residuum into the two categories of 'the deserving' and 'the undeserving' poor. But even the most experienced charity worker would probably have admitted that the distinction was a fine one. For example, if someone was suffering from chronic ill-health, it was not easy to decide if he had, at least to some extent, contributed to his own condition.

Helping the Residuum

The basic task, then, is easily defined: How could the residuum of the deserving and undeserving poor be persuaded to change their life-style and raise themselves out of that condition? Or, if it is accepted that some of them could or would *never* make the change, how should the residuum be assisted? In this approach the crux of the solution was, of course, *that only the residuum should be assisted, because only the residuum needed assistance.* Others had acquired the self-discipline which enabled them to develop a spirit of self-help and to provide for themselves by insurance despite their very modest incomes.

If the problem had been defined in this way, some answers would have been immediately eliminated, including the idea of universal 'benefits'. That the wives of millionaires and other highly paid people should be given a tax-free child benefit would rightly be regarded as absurd. All 'benefits' would be means-tested and directed to those who needed them. And even these 'benefits' would normally be temporary and combined with encouragement to take steps to make them unnecessary. Without this encouragement, the 'benefits' would quickly become 'detriments', since they led to the 'welfare' dependency which has become the curse of most advanced industrial societies and harmed the voluntary organisations (such as the friendly societies) through which self-help operated. When 'benefits' are provided 'free' by the state (in other words, paid for through the engine of compulsory taxation), few citizens will pay for similar benefits out of their own pockets.

Thus the emotional advocates of the massive expansion of state 'welfare' have won their case largely by the misuse of language. 'Welfare', which for most people should come mainly from their earned income and family relationships, is redefined as state hand-outs. And no mention is made of the result that regular hand-outs of this kind encourage 'welfare dependency' and moral degeneration.

State hand-outs are redefined as 'benefits', when their damaging long-term effects, both on the individuals who receive them and the voluntary societies which were previously so widely supported, should have been obvious. Moreover, we are repeatedly told that a further large expansion of state 'welfare' is necessary, when it is obvious that its ready availability is a primary cause of family breakdown and personal irresponsibility.

Grounds for Optimism?

So have the political and academic arguments already been lost? There are at least four reasons why the answer should be a firm 'No'.

- *First*, the publication of this collection of papers is good evidence that the debate is still open. The pen is indeed mightier than the sword, and a growing body of academic opinion is beginning to support radical reform of the 'welfare state'.

- *Second* is the continuing existence of numerous self-help agencies in the UK, despite the baleful influence of high taxation and the swollen state 'benefit' system. In 1991 the registered friendly societies still had over three million members and paid benefits of £261 million.

- *Third*, the tide of public opinion is beginning to accept some of these arguments. It was presumably that tide of opinion which persuaded Bill Clinton to promise to 'end welfare as we know it' during the 1992 election campaign, and as President of the USA he has recently (August 1996) signed a bill to make that promise effective. More recently in the UK Tony Blair, the leader of the Labour Party, has started to call for an end to the 'dependency culture'.

- *Fourth* is the careful research which could enable political leaders like Bill Clinton and John Major to devise acceptable plans for substituting real welfare for bogus welfare. The excellent report recently commissioned by the National Conference of Friendly Societies from George Yarrow, Fellow of Hertford College, Oxford, entitled *Social Security and Friendly Societies: Options for the Future*,[4] shows how the friendly societies could play a much larger part in a reformed social security system. And the second half of David Marsland's book, *Welfare or Welfare State?*,[5] provides a comprehensive and radical plan for welfare reform.

A Return to Self-Help?

But, even if the arguments in favour of self-help show signs of prevailing, will action follow? If the advocates of a massive expansion of state 'welfare' won their case during the 20th century, can there be grounds for supposing the tide can be 'rolled back' in the 21st? There are at least three good reasons for accepting that those who believe that self-help (including family and community support) is the best kind of help have time on their side.

First, there are the reports and publications of the past two years in the UK which indicate the intense interest in this topic and usually precede radical reform in a democratic society. The earliest of these – the report of the Social Justice Commission, chaired by Sir Gordon

---

[4] Discussed in Chapter 8 of this *Readings*.

[5] London: Macmillan, 1996.

Borrie – was published in October 1994. It produced wide-ranging proposals for welfare reform, including the taxation of some universal benefits (for example, child benefit) for those in the higher rate tax bracket. The chairman described his plan as 'the biggest shake-up of welfare for fifty years', and Mr Tony Blair described the report as 'a key contribution to the debate on second-generation welfare, which is about giving people a hand up and not just a hand-out'.

Nine months later the Commission on Wealth Creation and Social Cohesion, chaired by Lord Dahrendorf and established on the initiative of Mr Paddy Ashdown, leader of the Liberal Democrats, produced its report. Their focus was on 'maximising economic competitiveness while minimising its social cost'.

Meanwhile the Conservatives have had the task of administering policy while in office. The Minister most immediately concerned with the practical problems has been Peter Lilley, Secretary of State for Social Security. In 1995 a collection of his lectures and speeches delivered between 1993 and 1995 was published by the Social Market Foundation under the title *Winning the Welfare Debate*. Of course, in the light of the recent, steady increase in welfare expenditure this title might be considered somewhat optimistic, but the publication is worth reading. Perhaps the most interesting piece in it is Mr Lilley's 1993 Mais Lecture in which he advanced nine propositions about the reform of the social security system. The second of these was that 'any effective structural reform must involve either better targeting, or more self-provision, or both'. The last was that 'reform of something as vast as the social security system is best carried out sector by sector, rather than by the "big bang" approach', and he went on to say that this was his preferred approach to reform. Then he stated bluntly in his conclusion: 'Reforms of our welfare state are essential.'

These remarks were quickly followed by action. Late in 1994 the Government announced that a contractual 'Jobseekers Allowance' would replace Unemployment Benefit in 1996. After that, all unemployed people would be required to sign a Jobseeker's Agreement, setting out their availability for work and the steps they should take to look for it. Mr Lilley described the agreement as 'the taxpayers' bargain with the jobseeker that would make the system harder for the workshy'. While some members of the Opposition might wish to attack these proposals, others might agree that, given the growing acceptance that rights have to be balanced against responsibilities, they point in the right direction.

Thus leaders in all the main British political parties are now committed to reform of the welfare state, and academics and others of varied political views are joining in the debate. This is not a guarantee that reform will occur, but it suggests that something is going to happen. Some observers believe that seriously radical reform is more likely under a Labour government led by Mr Blair than under the present administration.

The *second* main factor which supports the reform movement is the fundamental changes in the global economy which are affecting the labour market in developed countries with an extensive welfare state. Of the Western European countries the UK has responded most effectively to these changes, but the USA is some way ahead of the UK.

The essence of these changes is the growing competition from low-wage countries in Central and Eastern Europe and the Far East which will become more intense in the next century. It leads to the shedding of labour by large firms as they become leaner and fitter, a growth in the number of part-time jobs (especially for women), and the expansion of employment in small- and medium-sized firms which cannot pay the same high wages and social costs as larger firms. Unless these changes take place, investment moves to low-wage countries, and the high-wage countries, like the member-states of the European Union, experience high and rising unemployment.

These changes in the global economy and the labour market mean that most people have to become more entrepreneurial. But a high-cost, high-tax welfare state does not easily fit with an enterprise economy. In this respect we see the US Congress giving a lead. 'The federal welfare system is to be closed down, transferring money – in diminishing amounts – along with responsibilities to the 50 states.'[6] Most surprisingly, the *American Prospect*, a left-leaning journal, wrote about this development that 'the affected groups, primarily women and children, have raised no significant resistance, nor has any protest been conspicuously mounted on their behalf'. The UK and other Western European countries do not have to copy the US model. But unless they move broadly in the same direction, their labour will become even more uncompetitive and unemployment rates – currently 10·5 per cent for the EU as a whole – will rise even higher. So reform is not an option – it is a necessity.

---

[6] Ambrose Evans-Pritchard, *Sunday Telegraph*, 1 October 1995.

The *third* good reason for optimism among those who seek radical reform concerns the massive social and economic changes in the UK and globally over the past 15 years. To begin with, there is the reform of trade union law and practice in the UK, which the experts told us was impossible when Mrs Thatcher decided to carry it through in 1979. Even the trade unions themselves have accepted that it cannot now be undone. Then there is the programme of privatisation which is almost complete in the UK and is now being copied by other countries all over the world. Who would have predicted 15 years ago that it could be taken so far? Finally, there is the collapse of communism, which took almost everyone by complete surprise. If communism can collapse, why should not its younger brother, the 'welfare state'?

Back to Samuel Smiles?

Reversion to a higher level of self-help, including personal pensions and other forms of individual insurance, does not necessarily mean a reversion to exactly the same kind of institutions which served our Victorian forebears well. The 21st century will be different from the 19th. But the spirit and ethos of Samuel Smiles, including the belief that no achievement is beyond those from the humblest backgrounds, remain the same. The 'tiger' economies of the Pacific rim seem determined to remain low-tax economies, in which the family is the mainstay of the welfare system. That attitude challenges the wealthy nations of Western Europe to abandon their welfare-dependency and recapture the spirits of enterprise and self-help which together created their original prosperity.

8

FRIENDLY SOCIETIES POISED TO EXPAND

George Yarrow
Hertford College, University of Oxford

IN THE 19TH AND EARLY 20TH CENTURIES friendly societies were the principal means by which millions of people sought to provide themselves with an element of security against contingencies such as sickness and death. Since then the societies have witnessed a long period of first relative and then absolute decline. Although today membership is still numbered in millions, friendly societies are only fringe contributors to the sum total of social insurance supplied in the UK.

The growth of both profit-seeking and mutual insurance companies over the same period was much healthier, but the decline of the friendly societies cannot be attributed to their displacement by these alternative suppliers in conditions of free competition. Rather, the societies' position in the market was steadily undermined by successive pieces of legislation that established and developed the state national insurance system, starting with the 1911 National Insurance Act.

Decline of the Friendly Societies

Since public and private insurance are (at least partial) substitutes for one another, the introduction of compulsory state schemes had adverse consequences for the demand for private provision. The impact on friendly societies was particularly severe because the societies' memberships were weighted towards the lower half of the income scale, and for many of their members even a relatively basic state scheme was regarded as providing all the protection they wanted.

The displacement of private provision by state schemes occurred in stages, with the major landmarks being the 1911 National Insurance Act and the legislation of the late 1940s. By introducing a *compulsory* state insurance scheme, the 1911 Act had the effect of reducing demand for the services supplied by friendly societies, but it did at least provide some compensation by establishing a rôle for the societies in the operation of the state scheme. More specifically, under the Act friendly societies (together with trade unions, collecting societies and industrial insurance companies) could, as 'Approved Societies', administer state sickness benefits.

Registered societies received management fees and payments from the state scheme for each contributor who enrolled with them. They were required to pay benefits on the scale prescribed by government, but efficient societies were able to generate additional surpluses that could then be paid out in additional benefits. Thus, common payments and fee scales led to a form of competition among societies to reduce costs,[1] but it is perhaps indicative of the spirit of the times that such incentives for efficiency were widely criticised because they tended to produce unequal benefits for equal contributions.

The advantages to friendly societies and their members of Approved Society status were not only the income provided from administration of state benefits and the associated opportunities to improve their financial position by increasing efficiency, but also the direct contact that administration of the state scheme gave with millions of potential members of the societies' other schemes. In effect, marketing costs were reduced by Approved Society status, helping to stimulate the overall level of private, 'top-up' provision in the market.

Beveridge sought to maintain the position of the friendly societies, among other things by preserving the rôle of the societies in the administration of sickness benefit and by arguing for a flat-rate contribution/flat-rate benefit system designed not to discourage incremental, personal provision. In his 1942 report, *Social Insurance and Allied Services*,[2] he recommended that the proposed Ministry of Social Security should make agreements with societies whereby they would act as agents for the administration of sickness benefit, provided that the relevant society met five conditions:

---

[1] More efficient societies tended to attract more members as a consequence of their higher benefits, while the less efficient tended to lose members. The arrangements have some economic similarities with recent reforms in the utility industries, where RPI-X regulation and yardstick competition (or competition by comparison) have been used to introduce greater incentives for efficiency.

[2] Cmnd. 6404, London: HMSO, 1942.

- it gave a substantial disability benefit from its own resources, that is, from the voluntary contributions of its own members;

- it had an efficient system of sick visiting of its members wherever they might be;

- it was effectively self governing;

- it did not work for profit, and was not associated with any body working for profit;

- it was registered under the Friendly Societies Acts or the Trade Union Acts, or, if not registered, it conformed substantially to the requirements for registration.

Beveridge's aims here were clear enough: to supplement state action with voluntary action in the form of additional disability benefits and a system of visiting the sick; to encourage membership of self-governing welfare organisations; and to try to ensure that non-state provision did not exploit those (often vulnerable) people on whom it was targeted. More generally, he argued that:

> 'The State in organising security must not stifle incentive, opportunity, responsibility; in establishing a national minimum, it should leave room and encouragement for voluntary action by each individual to provide more than the minimum for himself and his family.'[3]

In the event, however, Beveridge's proposals concerning friendly societies were rejected by the Attlee government in favour of full nationalisation of social security, and the societies therefore lost their rôle in the administration of the state system. Moreover, as the flat-rate contribution/benefit principle came to be abandoned in favour of means testing, the incentives for incremental, private provision by people of modest means were radically undermined. For example, in many cases means-testing removed virtually all of the benefits from small-scale personal savings and insurance policies.

Nor is this all: other government policies also had detrimental effects on friendly societies. Tax exemptions, for example, have distorted the savings market in numerous ways and, while friendly societies have

---

[3] Ibid.

been able to operate in their own 'tax efficient' niche in the market, they have inevitably suffered in this political game when compared with the much larger players which have more at stake financially. Similarly, in the most recent period, friendly societies have suffered from the costs imposed on them by a system of financial regulation that, whatever its merits and demerits, was largely designed to monitor and control other types of financial institution.[4]

As a result of these various policy developments, and in particular of the abandonment of the Approved Society approach and of the increased reliance on means testing, both the number and the membership of friendly societies fell dramatically in the post-war period.

Alternative Pasts

As Dr David Green has pointed out,[5] the 1911 National Insurance Act signalled the end of the liberal approach that had dominated government policy towards societies since the Friendly Societies Act of 1834. It is natural, therefore, to contemplate how the societies might have developed had the 1911 Act either:

- not been introduced at all, or

- taken a different form.

Of these two counter-factuals, the second is perhaps the easier to imagine, particularly since the draft legislation was substantially amended before it reached its final form.

Very many working-class members of friendly societies were opposed to the 1911 Act on the grounds that they were already covered by an insurance scheme and could not therefore see the point of being compelled to join the state system. Their preferred alternative was to be allowed to opt out of the state system, despite the potential benefits to them of the contributions paid into the state scheme by employers and by the Exchequer.

Opting out of state social security schemes is a policy option that is now very much back on the political agenda and it is not entirely

---

[4] Discussed in George Yarrow and Helen Lawton Smith, *Social Security and Friendly Societies: Options for the Future*, London: National Conference of Friendly Societies, 1993.

[5] David G. Green, *Reinventing Civil Society: The Rediscovery of Welfare without Politics*, London: IEA Health and Welfare Unit, 1993.

fanciful to contemplate the possibility of its adoption at the very outset of the state system. What, then, might have happened had the 1911 Act allowed individuals to substitute membership of approved, alternative schemes for membership of the new national insurance scheme?

It is likely that the state scheme would have enjoyed some success and that it would have taken significant business from the friendly societies. Given that the 1911 Act provided for contributions from employers and the Exchequer, the state scheme bundled together both pure insurance and income redistribution – in aggregate the employees covered by the scheme paid in less than they took out. The playing field for competition between government and private providers was, therefore, far from level: other things equal, the Exchequer contribution (funded from general taxation) was a benefit that could not be matched by non-state providers.

On the other hand, it seems equally clear that such a 'voluntary' state scheme would have had significantly less damaging consequences for the societies than did the compulsory scheme introduced in 1911. Many members of friendly societies would not have voluntarily switched to the state scheme, despite the potential gains from income redistribution, because of factors such as: attachment to the values embodied by friendly societies (such as independence and self-government); compensating efficiency advantages of non-state providers; higher quality of service of non-state providers; and the ability of smaller, competing organisations to offer arrangements better suited to individual circumstances.

Greater Strength

Given a combination of opting out and a rôle for friendly societies in the administration of the state scheme, a revised 1911 National Insurance Act might have led to a much more vigorous non-state sector in the subsequent decades. The membership of friendly societies in the 1920s and 1930s could have been expected to be significantly larger, and the extra coverage of the population, together with an opting-out precedent on the statute book, would have placed the societies in a more favourable position to influence later legislation.

It is unlikely that stronger friendly societies would have been able fully to resist the very powerful political pressures of the time for the development and extension of non-contributory, redistributive benefits. Nevertheless, an economically and politically stronger movement would have been a significant force in promoting legislation that would have had less damaging effects on the incentives for private provision, particularly by people with modest incomes. For example, one option that might have received more attention would have been for state income support to be channelled to the poor by means of subsidies for friendly society membership, with the societies then being responsible for the welfare of their members in the usual way. That is, state action on income redistribution could have been restricted to providing a genuine safety net, complementing the existing system of private provision rather than substantially displacing it.

Perhaps less speculatively, had the friendly societies been able to maintain their market position and political strength in the inter-war years, they would have been in a much better position to resist the near mortal blows inflicted on them by the legislation of the 1940s and after. As already explained, contrary to Beveridge's own recommendations this legislation not only fully nationalised the social security system by abandoning the Approved Society approach to benefit administration but also accorded a very major rôle to means-testing.

Although the Beveridge proposals for a universal and compulsory state scheme necessarily had damaging implications for friendly societies, non-state provision of savings and insurance products to lower-income households would today be on a significantly larger scale had Beveridge's recommendations on the administration of sickness benefits and on flat-rate benefits/contributions been fully adopted and maintained. The non-state sector would have been healthier still had opting out arrangements been introduced and preserved, and the dramatic post-war decline in the fortunes of friendly societies would then almost certainly have been avoided. The results of such developments would not only have been reduced pressure on the public finances from the social security budget but also a more diverse and innovative market-place for personal savings and insurance products.

To illustrate this last point, it can be noted that, historically, the institutions of welfare provision have taken a variety of forms. In the 19th century some friendly societies had branches and others did not; some were 'accumulating' societies, others were 'societies with dividends'. Among societies with dividends there were further sub-divisions into dividing societies, deposit societies and Holloway societies. These various institutional structures represented different approaches to the underlying social security problems of their members, and individuals were able to choose membership of the society or societies that most closely met their particular requirements. For example, a society targeted at a specific occupation could devise schemes appropriate to any special needs associated with that occupation.

Such diversity of approach is a major advantage of decentralised systems in a world in which the circumstances of individuals vary. Perhaps even more important in a society undergoing economic and social change, a multiplicity of competing providers means that there exists a breeding ground for innovation: new arrangements can be introduced in response to new demands, and innovations can quickly be 'market tested' on a small scale to identify those that are likely to be the more successful (which can then be copied and adopted more widely). All this was lost, however, as a consequence of the centralising and monopolising path taken by governments of differing political persuasions.

Alternative Futures: Resurrecting Voluntary Action?

The state welfare and social security system is now under long-term financial pressure as a result of a combination of factors that include cost escalation and voter resistance to higher taxation. Some retreat of the state from the social security arena can be confidently expected, although the nature and extent of that retreat are much more uncertain.

Given that it is likely that the state will continue to be concerned with the very poor, the groups most at risk from that withdrawal comprise those slightly higher up the income scale. This is because, for most of the 20th century, the state has systematically destroyed what had previously been the principal institutions through which these groups provided themselves with social security.

The awkward truth now is that, in current market conditions, simply reducing state provision of social security is unlikely to lead to a fully compensating increase in private provision on the part of low- and middle-income households. Having been weakened over the decades, friendly societies have been able to exert only very limited influence on key developments in taxation and regulatory policies. Although there have been some modest successes (such as aspects of the 1992 Friendly Societies Act), the policy environment is not favourable to the societies' resurgence.

As in the past, therefore, the future evolution of social security will be heavily dependent upon government policy choices. If social security budgets are cut and no further legislative action is taken, friendly societies would likely start to grow again. Growth would, however, be stunted by the inhospitable policy environment that has developed, cumulatively, since 1911.

If, therefore, there is a desire to see a renaissance of voluntary action in the provision of social security and social welfare – characterised by Beveridge as 'action not controlled or directed by the state ... a private enterprise for social progress'[6] – what is required is a more radical overhaul of the legislative framework, including reforms in taxation (of savings and insurance) and financial regulation. While voluntary action does not require special favours from the state in order to flourish, the history of friendly societies indicates that it would be greatly assisted by a liberal policy framework that does not discriminate against it.

---

[6] Speech in the House of Lords, *Hansard,* 22 June 1949.

9

CHARITY VERSUS THE STATE

Dennis O'Keeffe
University of North London

IN THE ECONOMIC AND SOCIOLOGICAL ANALYSIS of charity and the welfare state, imaginative counter-factual reasoning[1] is indispensable. Some scholars, such as A.J.P. Taylor, have argued that historical study should not engage in such speculation. They believe we should take Gibbon at his word and treat history as fundamentally a register of events to which we must always stick precisely.

This approach is unconvincing because it is inoperable. The core idea of Western civilisation is *freedom*, which implies that the human future is always open: accordingly, the past could have been different. How could we evaluate a law suit, a moral action, an individual life or an economic policy except by considering it relatively to what might have been?

The task is to separate good historical analysis from bad. A well-founded, enlightened counter-factual can lead to policies which enhance the quality of life. In the last century and a half of the two rival economic philosophies state economy arose as a challenge to the free market. Marxists and their allies urged the beneficial results alleged to flow from the replacement of free enterprise by socialism in the production of goods and services. Today, incontrovertible evidence reveals this reasoning as discredited. It was a fantasy which impoverished and enslaved human beings.

With the fall of communism, the free-enterprise idea demonstrates the counter-factual, in two ways. *First*, it is speculative history as an alternative to the statist version of recent reality. We may speculate on what the economic development of the former communist countries might have been but for the Marxist intervention.

---

[1] Defined and illustrated in the Preface.

Second, a counter-factual points the way out of the consequences of the Marxist interlude. Centralised state planning failed: let us try markets. This speculation is quite different from the Marxist dialectic. It leads to policies which enhance the quality of life. No wise social scientist will say that messes are easy to clear up; but in some post-communist countries, at least, emerging trends are supplying evidence favourable to the free enterprise system.

In free societies like Great Britain, the relevant question by definition is not 'How might free enterprise have managed the economic life of whole societies as opposed to socialist management?' It is rather the related question: 'In predominantly free-enterprise societies with large state-managed sectors, what results might have followed if they had been entrusted to private activity?' We should consider whether we too have lost by decades of state education, medicine and welfare. Not only has free enterprise been banished. One of the most important moral activities, private charity, has also been severely discouraged.

In the 20th century general socialism in the East was mostly inspired by Marxism. In the West, Marxism was mostly a minor input. Yet the inspirational error is the same. In both politicians and bureaucrats commit what Hayek calls the 'constructivist error' – the belief that state intervention can do better than the spontaneous activity of the market. And British sectoral socialism throws up powerful interest groups determined to fend off putative reform. A large class of functionaries would lose if private enterprise or private charitable activities were to displace the state. In some state welfare services, it is difficult even to suggest that alternative arrangements are conceivable.

The State versus Charity

All societies have poor and needy people. We may reasonably suppose that this will always be true, though modern free enterprise has normalised affluence. The question is what arrangements should be made for people whose standard of living and security fall, often through no fault of their own, below a minimum determined by consensus.

In the traditional cultures of pre-industrial Europe, most people were unimaginably poor by the standards of today. Most welfare 'needs' were met by private charity, mostly with direct church associations, the principal mechanism for welfare administration. In early modern Britain only two other private groups possessed enough wealth to make significant contributions to private charity: the aristocracy and the merchant class. Professor Wilber Jordan has shown the immense sums raised for charity by the bourgeoisie of Tudor England.[2] In modern Britain most people could (and many do) contribute to the relief of poverty or other distress.

During the 19th century there was an enormous increase in wealth, facilitating both a dramatic rise in real incomes and remarkable increases in the scope of privately funded welfare. The charitable life of the Victorians was expressed in the relief of poverty as well as in the encouragement of art and science. The world's first industrial society came into being with neither compulsory nor fully state-financed education, and with welfare arrangements depending either on private provision – as with the Friendly Societies – or on the generosity of private charity. The Scrooge model of our 19th-century ancestors is fictional.[3] Many of the 19th-century rich – and many not so rich – acted as if in agreement with Shakespeare's eulogy on individual mercy:

> '...It is twice blest,
> It blesseth him that gives, and him that takes.'

> (*The Merchant of Venice*, Act IV, Scene I)

The subsequent socialisation of British education, health and welfare was built up gradually by legislation and the extension of governmental writ, mostly before the First World War and after the Second. They not only largely banished free enterprise from welfare; they also significantly reduced the scope for private goodness.

Welfarism is expansionist, dragging private goods like education into state control. To get a real sense of the harm done, we must focus our analysis on the general *quantity, composition and quality* of services. Would a free market mean more or less education, health-care and support for the needy? What extra effects might charity have were the state curtailed and taxes cut? Would state or market reduce poverty more? The conclusions will depend on whether we think statically or dynamically.

Static and Dynamic Reckoning

A routine assumption is that masking prices by public finance increases demand. So do progressive taxes, the poor having higher marginal

---

[2] Wilber Jordan, *Charities of Rural England*, London: Greenwood, 1978.

[3] Arthur Seldon (ed.), *The Long Debate on Poverty*, IEA Readings No.9, London: Institute of Economic Affairs, 1972.

propensity to consume. If more consumption is held *ipso facto* desirable, some advocates will justify government provision.

The hostile view is that 'free' goods increase demand, but only through moral hazard. Hans Hermann-Hoppe says people demand more unemployment benefit, even choose unemployment, when government benefit is available. They may even want illegitimate children if the state pays for their upkeep.[4] Some speculative elements are apparent in these claims.

The idea that government provision must increase demand for services is static thinking. More welfare dependency will result. Even static thinking suggests an outcome different from the market version. We dynamise the analysis by allowing for variations in competition and efficiency. If services are priceless, welfarised 'demand' may mean careless misuse of resources. The more efficient market could manage the same output at lower cost.

Hermann-Hoppe is harsher. Socialisation leads to a *negative* utility, that is, the real economy is made smaller by the shift of resources from market to state, because the products are of lower quality.[5] Privatising education, health and insurance may increase the amount produced; but it would *certainly* improve their economic efficiency and quality.

If privatisation increased net income (after tax) sizeably, the effects would feed market demand. On the supply side, they would attract more suppliers. If higher quality production resulted, not only the real value of these services but even the volume of resources they use might increase. The economy would grow. There would be *more* well-educated and healthy people and *less* unemployment, less and better unemployment maintenance, with more beneficiaries who returned speedily to work which the market provides.

The parallel increase in private insurance, perhaps even with a revival of Friendly Societies, and the extra private charity flowing from lower taxes, would also feed their way into better education and health-care standards and superior support for citizens in temporary or long-term need. The state, partly freed from its colossal fiscal burden, could better help the minority of truly needy people.

Charitable giving must, like private spending, vary with net income. Unless we know the efficiency gap between state and market, the price

---

[4] Hans Hermann-Hoppe, 'Democratic Bankruptcy or Competing Governments?', in Nils Karlson (ed.), *Can the Problems of Mature Welfare States be Solved?*, Stockholm: City University Press, 1995, p.133.

[5] *Ibid.*, p.135.

and income elasticities of demand, the price elasticity of supply and the charitable propensities of higher net income, all of which affect the switch to private production, we cannot predict the overall *volume* effects of privatisation. Nevertheless, strong arguments point to a very definite increase.

Composition and Quality

Quality has been less debated than volume effects; but Hermann-Hoppe's argument emphasises the inferior quality of state production. Partial socialism implies, by contrast with full marketisation, inferiority in both the *composition and the quality* of output.

Private education, even if partly by charity, would be different from state education. Children would be better educated, as parents gained more leverage on the curriculum. We could expect rapid improvements in literacy and numeracy, and a flight from 'soft' social science – a dramatic shrinkage of the vast sociology estate. Consumer-power would trim faddish elements in education. The reversal of politically correct doctrines like anti-racism and multi-culturalism is probable; few people would 'buy' them if their price were visible. The composition of human capital would be recast in a technically more specific direction. Discursive study would remain predominant: that is the nature of education. Our civilisation would, nonetheless, be intellectually fortified by a market-led revival of 'tough' disciplines: traditional arts, history and science.

Comparable changes in the composition of medical output might be expected, with a marked improvement in technical efficacy as well as in economic efficiency. Some alternative medicine might achieve orthodox status, competing on more equal (market) terms.

With large reductions in income tax, an already generous society would give more to charity. The funds raised would affect not only the arts and sciences but all the services now trapped in the welfare state: education, medicine, social benefit, the relief of poverty and misfortune. Above all, the realm of individual responsibility would be extended.

Suppression of Civil Order

State-dominated societies have suppressed not only free enterprise but the whole civil order. A tragic aspect of government sectors in free societies is the way in which private charity has been curtailed by state action. Care for the less fortunate has been impoverished because it too has been socialised.

It is proper to ask what the world might have been like if the great charities, founders of so many almshouses, hospitals and schools, promoters of much admirable public spiritedness and learning, had been left to pursue their own course. How many schools, museums, sports grounds, theatres, hospitals, old folks' homes, and so on, might private goodness supply today if much of the ground were not pre-empted by state activity?

Society is still generous. It is also very rich.[6] Immense private sums are raised for famine relief, medical research and all sorts of educational purposes. And all this in an economy where the state appropriates more than two-fifths of Gross Domestic Product.

Imagine the possibilities for relief to the Exchequer, as well as for people in need, to say nothing of the increases in standards of living for those in work, if income taxes stood at no more than, say, 15 per cent. Private schooling and medicine would largely replace state production, leaving the state with the residual rôle of caring for the real unfortunates. Personal insurance would come into its own. And it would be genuine insurance, not the intemperate gobbling up of National Insurance contributions by improvident government. Above all, private charity would flourish.

Conclusion

Counter-factual analysis is essential to correct the history of statism. Radical trimming of the state would improve economic efficiency, with a net increase in volume of services and richer composition of output. Improvements in education and health would accompany reduced unemployment, destitution and dependency.

These advances signal an improved stock, and a re-ordered composition, of society's human capital. Insurance would be dramatically restructured. An expanded version of the Friendly Societies might take up a new rôle in the organisation of education and health as well as in insurance activity proper. Charitable giving would expand, with powerful consequences for all services which now shelter – often needlessly – beneath the state's umbrella.

Marketisation would affect alike the amount, composition and quality of output. Only when services have become sufficiently varied and they

---

[6] A small example: on 3 July 1994, the Oratory Church in London announced that its fete had raised £23,000 for the church restoration.

encounter ruthless market scrutiny, will those now under state control cater for subtly differentiated preferences. Without marketisation, huge sections of economic life will remain substandard.

Extending the scope of the capitalist economy will also permit, through its beneficial effects on post-tax incomes, a parallel improvement in the scope of private charity. This will simultaneously reinforce the improvements in material well-being produced by the market and re-establish the imperatives of the moral economy: the call to the individual to give for disinterested purposes.

Free enterprise, plus the free exercise of moral generosity by a mainly wealthy citizenry, paying low rates of taxes on middling and high earnings: that is the appropriate 'mixed economy' for the citizens of a free society.

10

THE POLITICAL PATH
OF TRANSITION

Nigel Ashford
University of Staffordshire

THERE IS NOW AN EXTENSIVE LITERATURE on the failure of the welfare state, and it is privately acknowledged by many politicians that extensive reform is required. Yet unlike the other pillars of the post-war collectivist consensus – Keynesian demand management and the mixed economy – it remains remarkably unaltered. While there are considerable efforts to improve its efficiency through managerial reforms and business practices, the rôle of the state in the financing and provision of welfare remains undiminished. The welfare state has so far been invulnerable to the intellectual onslaught against it, but there are intellectual-political strategies to overcome the obstacles to change.

Explanations for the strength of the welfare state emphasise either the power of ideas or of interests, part of a wider debate on the relative importance of ideas and interests in the determination of public policy.[1] These explanations are not mutually exclusive but will affect the choice of strategies most likely to prove rewarding, organised here under three headings: Exit, Voice and Loyalty.[2]

Resistance to Change: Ideas

Most studies attribute the successful resistance to change of the welfare state to the strength of its support amongst the electorate, as indicated in opinion polls. Ivor Crewe cites a poll in which 55 per cent declared as their ideal 'a society which emphasises the social and collective

---

[1] G. Jordan and N. Ashford, *Public Policy and the Impact of the New Right*, London: Pinter, 1993, pp.40-43.

[2] This borrows the title but not the substance of A. Hirschman's *Exit, Voice and Loyalty*, Cambridge, Mass.: Harvard University Press, 1970.

provision of welfare' compared with only 40 per cent in favour of 'a society where the individual looks after himself'.[3] Opinion polls appear to indicate support for the welfare state. Dennis Kavanagh notes that in a 1989 poll, 73 per cent of the public favoured increased expenditure on health, education and welfare, and only 10 per cent was for less taxation, with 14 per cent the same and 3 per cent don't know.[4] Polls are used by the welfare lobby to persuade politicians that any major reform would be electoral suicide.

These statistics are misleading:

- *First*, the welfare state means different things to different people. Intellectual defenders portray it as a system which provides an equal level of provision to all citizens, a mark of common citizenship. Its key features are equality and universality. Yet the public conception is that the welfare state should provide a reasonable degree of security for themselves and their families, and for others, through periods of sickness, unemployment, poverty and childhood, embodied in the metaphor of a safety net. This conception is characterised by security and compassion. The public wishes to see a society based on the latter principles, which does not require such an extensive state as the former.

- *Second*, these statistics are meaningless without prices.[5] IEA surveys demonstrate that support for increased expenditure rapidly declines when preferences are tested against proposed increases in taxes. This proposition is supported by experience. When faced with paying for increased expenditures in higher taxation, for example in 1993 and 1994, the electorate proved to be much less enamoured with paying more taxes.

- *Third*, these polls indicate that the public wants better health, education and welfare. In the current system, the only apparent means of achieving this for most people is through the state. The

---

[3] I. Crewe, 'Values : The Crusade that Failed', in D. Kavanagh and A.F. Seldon (eds.), *The Thatcher Effect*, Oxford : Oxford University Press, 1989, p.242.

[4] D. Kavanagh, *Thatcherism and British Politics*, Oxford: Oxford University Press, 1992.

[5] A.Seldon and R.Harris, *Welfare without the State*, Hobart Paperback No.26, London: Institute of Economic Affairs, 1987. The limitations of opinion polling are discussed in the Preface to this volume of *Readings*.

polls measure increasing expectations in these state services to match the improved quality and availability of private goods and services, not support for the principles of the welfare state. The polls also tap an increasing desire for product refinement, whereby consumers want the welfare product to match the variety of personal tastes and preferences, in direct contrast to the universal, 'one-size-fits-all' principle.

Any attempt to reform, let alone dismantle, the welfare state is always met by its defenders with the alarm call of fears that personal security will not be guaranteed, and that the poor and weak will be left to suffer. Any dismantling must meet the concerns of security and compassion, as suggested in the strategies discussed below.

Resistance to Change: Interests

Another significant block to change comes from powerful groups with a vested interest in maintaining the existing system, notably the service providers, and many of the direct beneficiaries. Failure to abolish the State Earnings-Related Pension Scheme (SERPS) was due mainly to the power of the trade unions, the poverty groups and insurance lobby, and the failure to introduce education vouchers mainly to the power of teachers' unions and their allies in the Department of Education.[6]

Employees of the welfare sector and their organised groups – the welfare lobby – have a strong vested interest in the employment, income and status provided by the welfare state. The National Health Service (NHS) is the biggest employer in Western Europe, with over 1 million employees, and 70 per cent of its expenditure is on salaries and wages. There are over 640,000 teachers. Producer groups, such as the British Medical Association (BMA), National Union of Teachers (NUT) and the British Association of Social Workers (BASW), are extremely powerful.

- *First*, they have a high density of potential membership.

- *Second*, they have detailed knowledge of their sector.

- *Third*, they are inevitably consulted before decisions are taken.

---

[6] SERPS is discussed by N. Barry in G. Jordan and N. Ashford, *op.cit.*, pp.251-67, and education vouchers in A.Seldon, *The Riddle of the Voucher*, Hobart Paperback No. 21, London: Institute of Economic Affairs, 1986.

- *Fourth*, they are the primary sources of opinion for the media on developments within their activities/field.

- *Fifth*, they are widely regarded as professionals, with a vocation, though this advantage is rapidly declining for some government sector workers such as social workers and teachers.

Another group of vested interests are the direct beneficiaries. About half of all people receiving a regular income obtain it from the state, either as salary or as transfer payments such as pensions and social security payments. Large numbers also benefit from 'free' services, such as schooling or dental treatment. The educated and articulate middle classes are the main beneficiaries of the welfare state. Goodin and LeGrand conducted an extensive survey of the class beneficiaries of welfare, and concluded that most services disproportionately favoured the higher-income groups, such as tax allowances on housing, post-16 education and the NHS.[7]

Some analysts insist that the failure of welfare reform can be attributed exclusively to the power of interests. Barry sees the maintenance of SERPS as 'a further example of the weakness of ideas...in the face of interest group pressure'.[8] This view ignores the interplay of ideas and interests. An individual's perception of personal interests is partly determined by his or her ideas. The working classes have not always believed that their interests are best protected by state control of their welfare; indeed, they frequently perceived it as a threat.[9] Ideas can support or undermine the power of interests. The influence of teachers over education policy, while extensive, is much less than in the past, as its public esteem has declined. As Barry acknowledges, 'the demystification of the old' is a necessary requirement if the veto power of the elderly in pensions policy is to be undermined.

Reformers who wish to diminish the rôle of the state in welfare must overcome resistance in the realm of ideas and interests: in ideas the desire for security and compassion, among interests the political

---

[7] R. Goodin and J. LeGrand, *The Middle Classes and the Welfare State*, London: Allen and Unwin, 1987, p.92.

[8] N. Barry, *op. cit.*, p.262.

[9] D. Green, *Working Class Patients and the Medical Establishment*, London: Temple Smith/Gower, 1984.

pressures of the welfare lobby and the direct beneficiaries. Strategies to achieve these results can be analysed as exit, voice and loyalty.

Exit

There must be maximum opportunities to opt out of state provision. Examples of exit are the sale of council housing to tenants, opting out of SERPS, and the growth of private health insurance. When asked to choose between contracting out, selective provision of the poor, or universal provision, the biggest group in the priced field surveys chose contracting out.[10] There is considerable untapped demand for contracting out, provided there is no double burden whereby people who provide for themselves have to pay as high taxes as those who fail to make their own provision.

Opting out has several advantages:

- *First*, the universality principle is undermined.

- *Second*, it provides for both security and compassion for people unable or currently unwilling to opt out.

- *Third*, it respects the differences in preferences and circumstances.

- *Fourth*, it creates a lobby for the protection and expansion of private provision.

- *Fifth*, it provides an opportunity for exit by service providers themselves, creating a lobby within the service.

More choice for consumers is frequently discussed, but rarely for the producer. As one of the biggest obstacles to reform is the existence of a powerful producer 'welfare lobby' that resists privatisation, employees within the government sector who are dissatisfied with the *status quo* must be identified and empowered. As well as exit for the consumer, opportunities for the producer to exit – for the nurse to work in a private hospital, for the teacher in a private school, or an academic in a private university – must also be created. There is a natural fear of change, and it may be necessary to compensate workers for change, as occurred with the free or cheap shares to employees in the privatised

---

[10] A. Seldon and R. Harris, *op.cit.*

companies. Whereas producer interest groups attribute problems to 'underfunding', some producers know that, given greater autonomy to make their own decisions and control their own resources, their drive and enthusiasm could produce a better service. This has been recognised in the success of Grant Maintained Schools. Chubb and Moe have identified the most important characteristics of a successful school as autonomy and a committed leadership.[11] Autonomy would lead to a desire to reduce dependence on the state even further. Instead of a united front of professionals hostile to privatisation, the media would see a diverse set of 'expert' opinions.

Voice

The undermining of interests by exit must be accompanied by a continuing critique of the ideological underpinnings of the welfare state – conceptually, economically, historically and comparatively.

- *First*, the conceptual distinction between the welfare state and the welfare society must be sharpened. The principles of the welfare state are: collectivism, redistribution, egalitarianism, the power of experts, and the existence of rights without obligations. The principles of the welfare society are: personal responsibility, security in troubled times through mutual aid, compassion for others, affiliation and bonding with social groups, and discernment in treatment between people in different circumstances.

- *Second*, the economic laws of scarcity demonstrate the meaninglessness of the idea of 'underfunding'. Welfare problems could not be 'solved' even if the whole of the GNP of the UK were spent on health or education. There is no clear relationship between expenditure and results, as evidenced by the substantial increase in expenditure since 1979 accompanied by ever-growing dissatisfaction. This failure of rising government expenditure has been demonstrated by numerous studies in the realm of education.[12]

- *Third*, the growing historical evidence of the existence of an extensive welfare society without the state in the 19th century needs

---

[11] J. Chubb and T. Moe, *Politics, Markets and America's Schools*, Washington DC: Brookings Institution, 1990.

[12] *Ibid.*, pp.102-104.

to be incorporated into the historical literature.[13] Most history books neglect the rôle of self-help groups such as the friendly societies or charities connected to businessmen and the churches. They also ignore the rôle of vested interests in the growth of the welfare rôle of the state. Even up to the 1970s charitable institutions had built over half the hospital places available.

- *Fourth*, more comparative analysis of welfare in other societies should be conducted to show how welfare can frequently be provided without the state. One of the features of the German social market system is its highly decentralised nature, with much provision in services such as health and welfare being supplied by insurance companies or voluntary and church-related groups. For example, 40 per cent of hospital beds are provided by voluntary (mostly church) organisations.

Loyalty

By loyalty is meant here the expression of compassion, a concern for the condition of others. Most people have a sense of obligation to the weak. This benevolent impulse cannot be expressed through the state because there is no relationship between the coerced taxpayer and the ultimate recipient. The original conception of compassion has become perverted by the modern state.[14] The market does not insist that every action or exchange must be profit-making, only that it must be non-coercive. There are numerous institutions for the expression of that impulse: families, friends, neighbourhoods, churches, charities, and voluntary associations. The family is the biggest provider of welfare, in the provision for children, the elderly and the sick. These institutions should be seen as the most appropriate moral outlet for these obligations, rather than organising demands for more state expenditure. Unfortunately, the growth of the state has undermined these institutions, displacing them as the main providers of welfare.[15] It has also undermined the sense of personal obligation when people are

---

[13] E.G.West, *Education and the State*, London: Institute of Economic Affairs, 2nd edn., 1970, 3rd edn., Indianapolis, IN: Liberty Fund, 1994; A. Seldon, *Capitalism*, Oxford: Blackwell, 1990; D. Green, *Reinventing Civil Society*, London: IEA Health and Welfare Unit, 1993.

[14] M. Olasky, *The Tragedy of American Compassion*, Chicago: Regnery Gateway, 1992.

[15] N. Glazer, *The Limits of Social Policy*, Cambridge, Mass.: Harvard University Press, 1988, Ch. 1.

willing to shift responsibility for assisting their family, friends and neighbours onto the state.

The Politics of Welfare Without the State

If the welfare state had never been created, welfare would be the responsibility of a large number and variety of profit-making, mutual aid and charitable institutions. In the realm of ideas, everyone would accept that competition in welfare services is desirable, not only on grounds of efficiency but also of flexibility towards varied wants. There would be strong and diverse opinions over the most appropriate methods of service provision, but rather than seek to impose a uniform system, institutions would compete to demonstrate the superiority of their own approaches. There would be debate over whether there was sufficient competition. Do regulations protect consumers or restrict the entry of new firms offering more flexible and innovatory services? Do the tax and other advantages of charitable organisations create 'unfair' competition with profit-makers?

In the realm of interests, the welfare professionals would compete for clients and their life-time employment, retirement, health and education accounts. Producer groups would, as always, seek to manipulate laws to promote their own interests. Small companies would demand stronger anti-trust laws to break up giants. Big companies would want stricter regulations to put smaller competitors out of business. Yet none would be very successful in its efforts.

- *First*, the process would be more transparent, as the welfare industry would be outside the formal structure of the state.

- *Second*, the industry would be divided and competing suppliers would act as countervailing influences.

- *Third*, politicians would know that any interference in the market would be opposed by at least some groups, who would command the loyalty, confidence and trust of their members, far more than would the politicians.

- *Finally*, the customers themselves would have more access to information about the activities of the welfare institutions and more awareness of the politics of special interests. Competing morality indexes would monitor the political activities of the welfare industry and publish information about their anti-consumer activities, when they sought to regulate prices or exclude competition. Consumers would be quick to move their business away from welfare groups which engaged in such activities.

The welfare state exists, but so do some elements of a welfare society. The provision of welfare is already a mixture of state, market and household.[16] Universal and egalitarian principles have never been as widely accepted or implemented as its advocates would believe. The boundaries of welfare can shift away from the state in favour of market and household. Any strategy to privatise the welfare state must identify the obstacles, in the realms of ideas and interests, and present a variety of strategies in exit, voice and loyalty.

---

[16] R. Rose and R.Shiratori (eds.), *The Welfare State: East and West*, Oxford: Oxford University Press, 1986.

11

THE VERDICT OF HISTORY

Arthur Seldon

THE WELFARE STATE IS essentially a political artefact. Its origins lie in the party politics of the Victorian era. It was presented by the competing Liberals and Conservatives as an act of communal compassion in alleviating the condition of the poor, especially the enfranchised working classes. The state was not the only source of welfare and it had obvious defects. But from its symbolic beginning with the Education Act of 1870 to 'fill the gaps' left in some towns by the growing private schools, it has been extended over the past century to provide medical care, housing (for several millions), pensions, insurance for unemployment, and much else for everyman and his wife and children. The implicit political judgement on everyman today is that he is less competent, less responsible and less provident than his great-grand-father who managed on a tithe of his earnings.

The purpose of this collection of essays is to attempt the rare exercise of judging the benefits of the welfare state by counting its costs. Macro-economic financial cost conveys little of its real-life cost in the sacrifice of the varied systems that would have developed in the open market from the mid-19th century.

The 'counter-factual' applies historical judgement to assess the alternatives that the chance confluence of circumstance, the 'accidents' of history, displaced. There is much unquestioning approval of the benefits of the welfare state: its compassion for the poor, the homeless, the sick, the indigent in old age. Yet its contribution to civilised living cannot be judged solely by its achievements. They were made with massive resources that could have been used in other ways that even scholarly histories often ignore and imply would not have emerged or been developed to suit the changing times.

Historians conventionally study 'history', understood generally as the developments that took place. Dynastic, constitutional, political, military histories are often qualified by judgements on the better decisions the chief players *might better have made*, the mishaps avoided, the happier results that might have followed. Yet 'social' histories rarely pause to count the opportunity cost of the welfare state in the better welfare it suppressed.

Their judgements would have been more productive if they had studied rather less the decisions of political power in government and rather more the *potential* economic power of the common people. The majority decisions of the political process usually submerge minorities and individuals who would be heeded more effectively in the market. The power of government is constrained and, in the end, it can be over-ridden by the market, as the welfare state is being replaced by more responsive competitive services in the approach to the 21st century.

Historical Evidence

Three other historical approaches are irrelevant or inconclusive: comparison, or rather contrast, with the embryo private alternatives emerging in the mid-19th century, with the mature but government-restricted alternatives in the late-20th century, or with the younger societies of the former British Dominions. The most relevant material available to objective scholars for historical judgement is the ample evidence presented in this book on the early services and institutions most likely to have expanded if they had not been repressed.

First, recent researches into the early history of education, medical care, housing, saving for old age and retirement, reviewed in Chapters 2 to 8, reveal the voluntary early efforts of families to provide themselves with all the main elements of the welfare state.

Second, the very large expansion in incomes since the 1860s would have been available to pay in the market if people had been free to continue and develop their responses to the private (often church) schools, medical benefit insurers, and, later, homes for sale and personal pensions.

Third, rising discretionary expenditures on the improving quality and widening range of food and clothing, amenities and luxuries were available more readily and earlier to the wealthier who could pay both the taxes and the prices for education and medical care still now largely denied to the working classes by compulsory state welfare that is more responsive to the better-connected middle classes.

Fourth, the welfare state was inflated by its controllers and staffs. The economics of politics, inspired by the Scottish and English classical liberal philosophers, and refined by the American school of public choice, clearly points to its micro-economic political temptations. Politicians acquired widening power. The bureaucracy inflated its growing empire. The professional associations of doctors, teachers, nurses, public administrators, and trade unions of clerical and manual workers found easier 'rent-seeking' from government monopolies spending taxpayers' money than from competing mutual fraternities spending their members' money or from profit-earning suppliers and insurers risking their shareholders' money.

Scholars are here in the realm of exchanging reasoned judgement. There can be no confident exclusion of the probability that the welfare state has entailed horrendous 'cost' in the lost services that would have grown to serve the mass of the people. There is no convincing or decisive reason to suppose that they would have ceased to develop more responsive private education, medical care, housing, saving, pensions, insurance for unemployment and much else 'tailored' for individuals, trades, professions, communities.

The balance of probability points to their expansion under the influence of innovators and entrepreneurs tested in competition and then trusted by people who knew their local society and branch managers. Such local associations and communities rested on fraternal understanding and sympathy based on loyalties of neighbourhood, district and religion foreign to the best intentions of the state. This was the spontaneous evolution of community that grew from the bottom rather than the spurious communitarian imposition by political coercion from the state at the top.

Members of mutual organisations would then have remained until today 'brothers'. Or they would have emerged as sovereign consumers – 'customers' who could escape from inadequate suppliers. Instead they are 'beneficiaries' – state school 'parents', NHS 'patients', council 'tenants', state 'pensioners' without individual power to bargain or escape, and, if working class, often supplicants.

British Rail has replaced direct-paying (though often taxpayer-subsidised) 'passengers' by 'customers'. The welfare state fights shy of 'customers' who pay indirectly by taxes. The anxious reasoning of its managers is understandable. 'Customers' would not have accepted 'national curricula' framed by far-off civil servants little concerned about family instinct and affection. 'Customers' would have resented long waiting for hospitals run by administrators answerable to government or professional associations. 'Customers' would not have tolerated council housing or tower blocks controlled by councillors sensitive to trade unions. 'Customers' would hardly have accepted state pensions manipulated by Westminster politicians for party advantage.

Welfare State Is Socially Divisive

The welfare state has intensified the divide between the middle classes who pay for what they choose and the working classes who mostly have to content themselves with what they are given by the state. It has retarded the social merging evident in more mobile Western societies undivided by the British 'national' health and other 'public' services.

Both government and the market are prone to 'failures'. The market, as Professor Jackson illustrates, has had three main 'problems' of adverse selection, moral hazard and agency. The crucial and debatable question for historians is whether or how far the market would have discovered its characteristic solutions.

Economists have been devising methods of removing market 'imperfections'. And governments in some countries have increasingly adopted their thinking, replacing state by private services, partly for political motives though probably more for economic reasons. State services have been found unpopular because tax rejection has reduced government funds and lowered quality.

Even with the lower incomes in the developing countries Dr Gabriel Roth, in a research study for the World Bank, found that they had been evolving private innovations in the supply of 'public' services.[1] They were able to overcome the 'public goods' and 'free rider' obstacles, once considered inherent barriers to the market supply of education, medical care, water and sewerage, and communication services. And they have found ways to meet the exceptional circumstances of people with the lowest incomes. More recently Dr Fred Foldvary, for the American Locke Institute, has developed methods of competitive supply of 'public' goods in advanced countries.[2]

And Chile, a country that has faced the acute problems of encouraging economic growth in a developing country, is teaching lessons to the developed West by demonstrating new devices for privatising erstwhile state welfare services in social security, medical care, higher education, local government, and communications.[3]

---

[1] G. Roth, *The Private Provision of Public Services*, Oxford: Oxford University Press, 1987.

[2] Fred Foldvary, *Public Goods and Private Communities: The Market Provision of Social Services*, Aldershot: Edward Elgar Publishing, 1994.

[3] Cristian Larroulet (ed.), *Private Solutions to Public Problems: The Chilean Experience*, Santiago, 1993.

Government or Market? Choice or Restriction

An analysis of the relative achievements and failures of collective (government) and individual (market) choice leads Professor Richard Wagner of George Mason University in Virginia, writing in the methodology of 'public choice' (better described as the economics of politics), to oppose 'the welfare state' against 'the general welfare'.[4] He emphasises the constitutional difference between limited ('contractarian') government, in which the legislators cannot suppress the scope for the market to produce welfare, and 'unlimited' ('majoritarian') government in which voter majorities are able to suppress minority or independent initiatives.

It would seem that the argument rests with the open, if less tidy, system that allows experimentation rather than with the tidier but restrictive system that excludes or inhibits it by demanding political conformity. It has, as a major example, long been considered that insurance against the risks of unemployment is a case for state organisation on the apparently clear ground that the decision to be 'unemployed' is subject to moral hazard because the individual can, for physical and even more subjective psychological reasons, reject offers of employment and claim the insured sums of money. In this book Professor Beenstock demonstrates the principles on which moral hazard could be tested by objective experience such as seasonal trends in unemployment and insurance offered in the market by competing insurers.

On comparable grounds, it is plausible to argue that all state welfare services could be open to constant comparison with possible private alternatives to decide which is the better for the public. Not least, state education could be under constant test to ensure that it meets the preferences of parents.

Further alternatives, such as delivering monopoly state services by competing private suppliers, or financing them by prices rather than taxes, have been explored in recent years.[5] The obstacle is essentially

---

[4] Richard Wagner, *To Promote the General Welfare*, Pacific Research Institute for Public Policy, San Francisco: CA, 1989.

[5] Vincent and Elinor Ostrom, 'Public Goods and Public Choices', in E.S. Savas (ed.), *Alternatives for Delivering Public Services*, Colorado: Westview Press, 1977. The advantages of direct charging by prices in place of indirect financing by taxes are discussed in A. Seldon, *Charge*, London: Maurice Temple Smith, 1977, and in Richard Wagner (ed.), *Charging for Government*, London: Routledge, 1991.

that government can protect its services from open comparison. Experiments in the voucher system were suppressed by the Conservative Government in 1983 largely because it was opposed by vested interests, mainly in the teacher trade unions, that preferred to be employed (ultimately) and their remuneration decided nationally by the state rather than by parents with bargaining power based on the payment of school fees. It is difficult to argue that parents, especially those with the lower incomes, have gained from the suppression of the opportunity to compare schools and move freely between them.

The crucial weakness is not so much in the market as in the political process. The most intractable obstruction to reform is not so much moral as political. The failures of government that must be set against the failures of the market are considerable. The test of the relative significance of government and market 'failures' is less in their frequency than in the ease with which they can be escaped. The natural recuperative powers of the market induce competing private suppliers to find ways to reduce their defects earlier than the state monopoly. The market discovers the 'scoundrels' sooner.

The state has suppressed the price mechanism in schooling and medicine without creating a better method of valuing resources. It has weakened the family by usurping the rôle of parents in schooling, medical care, and, still in the 1990s for millions, in housing. The state has based its welfare policies on their income-effect and neglected their price-effect on incentives to make the most of natural or acquired abilities. The financial differences that decide access in the market have been replaced by cultural differences of personal accent and social connections that are more difficult to offset in deciding access to the state. It has distorted individual life-patterns by responding to immediate personal producer interests at the expense of long-term personal consumer interests.

Conclusions: State Imperfections and Future Demands and Innovations

The imperfections of the state have remained concealed for decades up to and exceeding half a century. The state prevents the market from discovering the imperfections of the welfare state and the remedies. To prove itself, state welfare must be open to competing methods of production. In the last resort it must return its taxes for dissatisfied consumers to spend as they wish on private services at home or overseas.

The decisive probabilities are three:

- *First*, as incomes rise, more people are being enabled to escape from the welfare monopolies both at home and, for medical care and saving, increasingly overseas to the single market in Europe and to the world market enlarged by the World Trade Organisation. The finally emerging working classes are growing impatient with their relatively poor state schooling and medical care.

- *Second*, accelerating innovation will supply new methods of producing consumer-oriented welfare services beyond the capacity of centralised, standardised, bureaucratised government. Education and medical care no longer require universally large buildings called schools and hospitals that the state will preserve too long.

- *Third*, both supply and demand will be reinforced by the state itself, which induces more people to reject the offensive taxation it demands to pay for unsatisfactory services. Conventional tax rejection is being increasingly supplemented by the barter that eludes official measurement even more than tax avoidance and evasion.

The case for continuing or expanding the national welfare state is weakened by its incapacity to determine the decisions of people who can escape to international markets. If the political process cannot produce modernised welfare services because it is prevented by ideological faith in the state, by bureaucracy, and by vested interests, the market process will replace it because its remaining defects will become more remediable or loom less large than its suitability for the 21st century. Then the British will be one nation of consumers in buyers' markets in welfare. That, in the end, would seem the verdict of history.

Markets and the Media

Competition, Regulation and the Interests of Consumers

Governments, faced with problems which elicit public concern, are all too ready to pass restrictive legislation, establish supervisory committees and commissions, or pass difficult issues to regulators of particular sectors of the economy. In the course of time, the probable outcome is a huge regulatory edifice, involving massive compliance costs for firms and individuals, and striking at the roots of economic change by severely hindering entrepreneurship.

The 'media' industries in all their forms are favoured candidates for regulation. Governments seem unwilling to let markets in media work, claiming 'imperfections' and 'failures' which require regulation.

But what substance is there in these claims? To what extent is regulation feasible, given that technological advance is blurring the dividing lines among different forms of media? And are there such problems in the media – for example, concentrations of power through dominant owners – that market processes cannot be trusted to protect consumers?

IEA Readings 43, edited by Michael Beesley, explores such questions. Professor Beesley introduces the volume, summarising and commenting on the views of the other contributors. The following four chapters deal with specific issues in media regulation – copyright by Dan Goyder, digital technology and its implications by Malcolm Matson, the future of public service broadcasting by David Sawers, and concentration and diversity by William Shew and Irwin Stelzer.

Contents

ISBN: 0-255 36378-8

IEA Readings 43

£16.50
incl. p&p

The Institute of Economic Affairs
2 Lord North Street, Westminster
London SW1P 3LB
Telephone and sales: 0171 799 3745
Fax: 0171 799 2137

Regulating Utilities: A Time For Change?

Now that privatisation of utilities is substantially complete, regulation has become a major economic and political issue.

To provide an intellectual basis for utility regulation, each year the Institute in conjunction with the London Business School publishes a set of *Readings* which assesses the state of regulation, considers what problems have arisen, and discusses how they might be solved, taking into account the experiences of other countries. The authors adopt no common political or ideological stance: they bring a variety of viewpoints to bear since the intention is to stimulate debate.

The 1996 edition of this comprehensive and up-to-date review of utility regulation in Britain includes contributions not only from academic commentators but from the utility regulators and the heads of the general competition authorities.

Contents

ISBN: 0-255 36381-8   IEA Readings 44

£18.50
incl. p&p

The Institute of Economic Affairs
2 Lord North Street, Westminster
London SW1P 3LB
Telephone and sales: 0171 799 3745
Fax: 0171 799 2137

SHOULD DEVELOPING COUNTRIES
HAVE CENTRAL BANKS?

KURT SCHULER

1. Central banking, though now widespread, is a relatively recent phenomenon, especially in developing countries.

2. Rivals to central banking include currency boards, monetary institutes, free banking, and 'dollarisation'.

3. Most economists and policy-makers believe every independent country should have its own central bank so it can conduct an independent monetary policy.

4. This study, for the first time, shows how central banking in developing countries has performed relative to other monetary systems in developing countries and to central banking in developed countries.

5. Measures of economic growth and 'currency quality' (such as inflation rates, periods of high inflation, exchange rates) for 155 countries are analysed to provide performance indicators.

6. The results show clearly that '...central banking in developing countries has performed worse than other monetary systems and worse than central banking in developed countries'.

7. Moreover, these results are robust. Other methods of analysis or classification would be unlikely to change the conclusions.

8. Central banking continues to spread in the developing world mainly because of the consensus in its favour among economists and policy-makers.

9. 'Political opportunism' also plays its part: central banks will '...more readily finance government budget deficits than more rule-based monetary systems'. Furthermore, central banks '...can be formidable political lobbies'.

10. According to this study most developing countries would have been better off importing monetary policy. Some have recently established currency boards: others should follow their example.

ISBN 0-255 36382-6   Research Monograph 52   **£11.00**
incl. p&p

THE INSTITUTE OF ECONOMIC AFFAIRS
2 Lord North Street, Westminster
London SW1P 3LB
Telephone: 0171 799 3745
Fax: 0171 799 2137

Better Off Out?

BRIAN HINDLEY and MARTIN HOWE

1. A majority of other member states may insist on a 'federalist' agenda for the EU that a British government (of either party) would find unacceptable.

2. If that occurred, the economic costs and benefits of EU membership would be crucial in determining Britain's response.

3. Britain has the effective legal power to secede from the EU: Parliament could terminate the enforceability of Community Law in the British courts. Withdrawal would more likely be by agreement than by a 'messy unilateral break'.

4. Outside the EU, Britain might become a free-standing member of the world trading system, relying on WTO trading rules. More likely there would be some form of free trading relationship with the rest of the EU.

5. Many costs and benefits of EU membership are intangible. For instance, Britain may suffer from excessive EU regulation and from the more effective enforcement of single market and other rules in British courts than elsewhere.

6. An assessment of those costs and benefits which can be quantified suggests the net effect of withdrawal on the British economy would be small – probably less than 1 per cent of GDP. If a special relationship with the rest of the EU were arranged, there might be a small benefit.

7. The major quantifiable cost of EU membership is adherence to the Common Agricultural Policy (CAP). Escape from the CAP would represent a clear gain to Britain.

8. There would be some loss because of the imposition of tariff barriers on UK exports to the EU but, allowing for switching of exports to non-EU countries and other adjustments, it would be small.

9. Some loss of inward foreign direct investment (FDI) might also occur, though Britain's flexible labour markets (rather than EU membership) may be the principal reason for much FDI.

10. There is no foundation for the idea that UK departure from the EU would have 'dire economic consequences'. 'If the EU ...develops along lines that the UK finds unacceptable on fundamental political grounds, fear of adverse economic consequences should not deter a British government from seeking to change the relationship of the UK with the EU or, in the last resort, from leaving the Union.'

ISBN 0-255 36388-5

IEA Occasional Paper No.99

The Institute of Economic Affairs
2 Lord North Street, Westminster
London SW1P 3LB
Telephone and sales: 0171 799 3745
Fax: 0171 799 2137

£9.00
incl. p&p

IEA